ACKNOWLEDGEMENTS

This book would not have been possible without the volunteers on the Staffordshire Appeals Project based at Staffordshire and Stoke-on-Trent Archive Service. They are: Phil Adams, Judy Aston, John Babb, Gerry Barton, Kathryn Barton, Richard Benefer, Melanie Bond, Pat Brown, Ann Bugge, Quentin Butler, Mary Carpenter, Allen Cook, Val Cooper, Caroline Hillman, Douglas Crump, Jenny Crump, Christine D'Agostino, Judith Gilbert, Eleanor Grigson, Claire Hannon, Doug Henderson, Christine Hill, Lydia Hodkinson, Val Hollins, Ruth Humphreys, Valerie Kremer, John Leech, Martin Livette, Christine Miller, Irene Moir, Linda Moseley, Kathy Niblett, Kelly Norman, Lyn Norman, Neil Norman, Denise Peel, David Price, Ceris Roberts, Dave Rogers, Rose Sawyers, Ruth Shaw, Ian Small, Allison Smith, Stephen Smith, William Tapper, Wendy Thain, Tom Thornton, Dave Whitehead, Jennifer Williams, Ray Wilson, Vicky Wood and Natasha Yardley. Rachael Cooksey was an enthusiastic Project Officer who held everything together while Matthew Blake, Participation and Engagement Officer, Archives & Heritage, has been on this journey right from the beginning.

I am particularly grateful to those who commented on chapters: John Babb, Gerry Barton, Ben Benefer, Matthew Blake, Val Cooper, Irene Moir and Rose Sawyers.

Thanks also go to:

Heritage Lottery Fund for funding the original work of volunteers on the Mid-Staffordshire Appeals Tribunal papers and their context (https://staffsappeals1918.wordpress.com).

The Everyday Lives in War: First World War Engagement Centre (https://everdaylivesinwar. herts.ac.uk), which provided a grant for Professor Karen Hunt to work with the project (The Mid Staffordshire Appeals Tribunal: a window onto everyday life on the Staffordshire home front).

Staffordshire Archives & Heritage Service and the Trustees of the William Salt Library for permission to reproduce images from their collections, many of which are available at www.staffspasttrack.org.uk, and Howard Dixon for producing high-resolution images. All images, unless otherwise indicated, come from Staffordshire Archives & Heritage.

Suzy Blake for the map of Staffordshire.

Fenella Webster and her family for kindly allowing access to Edith Birchall's diary.

And on a personal note, to all at Amberley Publishing for being so understanding; to all my new friends in Bridport who have remained curious about this project; and most of all my thanks and love to Colin Divall, who has had to live with this book for far too long.

A note about money:
As a very rough guide, £1 in 1914 would be worth £106 at 2016 prices while by 1919 £1 was only worth £47 (Bank of England's inflation calculator, www.bankofengland.co.uk).

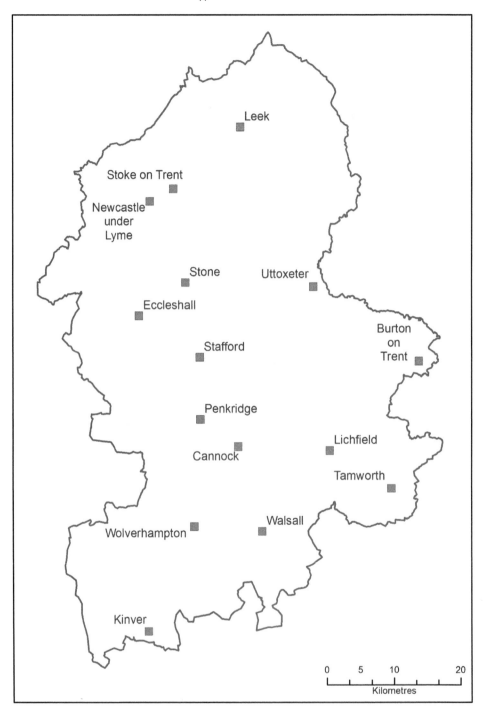

Map of Staffordshire, *c.* 1914.

Voices of the First World War

STAFFORDSHIRE'S WAR

Karen Hunt

AMBERLEY

First published 2017

Amberley Publishing
The Hill, Stroud
Gloucestershire, GL5 4EP

www. amberley-books.com

British Library Cataloguing in Publication Data. A catalogue record for this book is available
from the British Library.

ISBN 978 1 4456 5785 1 (print)
ISBN 978 1 4456 5786 8 (ebook)

Origination by Amberley Publishing.
Printed in the UK.

CONTENTS

ABOUT THE AUTHOR

Karen Hunt is Professor Emerita of Modern British History at Keele University and former Chair of the Social History Society. She is a gender historian and has published widely, including *Equivocal Feminists* (1996) and, with June Hannam, *Socialist Women* (2002). Her work on the First World War home front includes studies of women and the politics of food, the housewife, and gender and everyday life across the home fronts of the world. She was an adviser to the BBC's World War One at Home project in the West Midlands, working with journalists to produce a 100 local stories of the home front which were broadcast in 2014.

INTRODUCTION

On 13 August 2014 Staffordshire in the First World War made the national news headlines on radio and television. What had caught people's attention was the announcement of the unusual survival of a full set of papers from one of the tribunals that adjudicated on many cases of men who sought exemption from military service after conscription was introduced in Britain in 1916. Staffordshire and Stoke-on-Trent Archive Service had been awarded a Heritage Lottery Fund grant to open up to the public the papers of the Mid-Staffordshire Military Service Appeal Tribunal. They were looking for volunteers to help.

Among the personal papers of Eustace Joy (1867–1940) in Staffordshire Record Office was an extensive set of records that should not have been there. Joy had been the most senior public servant in the county in the first decades of the twentieth century as Clerk to Staffordshire County Council from 1907 to 1933. In the First World War he had been one of the military representatives who advised local Military Service Tribunals about the Army's requirements and brought appeals on behalf of them to the local Appeal Tribunal. Joy had saved all the bureaucratic material – completed forms and supporting correspondence – for every case heard by one of Staffordshire's three Appeal Tribunals. The tribunals had the power to decide whether individual men could be exempted temporarily or absolutely from military service or must accept their immediate call-up into the Army. After the war, the government ordered all tribunal material to be destroyed with the exception of two examples: Middlesex and Peebles and Lothian Appeals Tribunals. It was feared that opening up the sensitive decisions of the tribunals to public scrutiny could be explosive in the immediate post-war world. However, their destruction was also ordered because the extensive paperwork demanded by a national system of tribunals that ran from 1916 to 1918 contained personal details of the men who sought exemption and the effect that the war was having on them, their families and businesses. It is this aspect of the Appeals papers that has so much potential for understanding what it was like to live in Staffordshire during the First World War.

The paperwork associated with the Local and Appeal Tribunals provides a glimpse not only of the individual lives of men of military age, but also their families and their workplaces. We can learn how the war had already been experienced up to the point of a man's conscription and how they, their households and workplaces had responded to the demands that the war made on them. Widening research, particularly to the extensive and informative local press, it is possible to track how local communities experienced these unpredictable and challenging times. Drilling down into the experience of the men, women and children who lived in wartime Staffordshire, it becomes clear that how they dealt with the stresses of everyday life might make the difference not just to their individual survival but also to that of their community, county, and, ultimately, country. This gives us a different perspective on the First World War.

This book was made possible by the chain of events started by the publicity produced that August day in 2014. The call for volunteers to open up the Appeals papers and the associated boxes of Joy's correspondence produced a much greater response than anticipated. The idea had been to digitise the Appeals case files and catalogue the correspondence. Now it was

Portrait of Eustace Joy, 1933.

possible to explore a wide range of local sources to contextualise the Appeals papers and to begin to understand what they revealed not just about how the tribunals operated but also about life in wartime Staffordshire. Local newspapers, school log books, diaries and letters as well as official records were all examined. Indeed, so much material was collected that the next issue was how to make sense of it all. A grant from the Everyday Lives in War: First World War Engagement Centre enabled Professor Karen Hunt to work with the HLF Appeals project to analyse the new material that had been unearthed and to begin to identify the different kinds of stories that could now be told about the war if the focus was on life at home in Staffordshire.

Far away from the trenches of the First World War, people in Staffordshire were not only affected by the country's overseas battles, but were also participants in the war. This book looks at what it was like to be part of the first home front in the new phenomenon of 'total war'. This novel kind of warfare mobilised unprecedented numbers of men from across the world to fight but it also depended upon the organisation and resilience of a new and equally important 'front' in each belligerent nation. This was the home front. It comprised all civilians: women and men, young and old, whether they were inhabitants of cities, towns or rural villages. To fight this new kind of modern warfare, a belligerent not only had to arm its fighting men, it had to organise itself to feed an army at the front and maintain a healthy civilian population to maximise war production to equip that army.

One of the crucial sites for this new kind of warfare was the daily life of ordinary people at home in places like Staffordshire. Creating and sustaining a home front was a new venture for Britain, as for the other belligerents. What became increasingly clear as the war developed was how important the home front was to the successful prosecution of the war. Each nation

The banner behind the munition workers and band of Siemen's, Stafford, sums up the idea of a home front: 'Women work while the men fight'.

had not only to keep providing men to replace dead and wounded soldiers, it also had to organise itself to equip and feed an army at the front. At the same time this could only be achieved by sustaining a civilian population to work long hours needed to produce not only the shells but the uniforms, the food and everything else needed by the military. That meant that there also had to be enough food and fuel to maintain health, and, as importantly, morale of the civilians. It was essential to keep the support of the people if the hardships of the home front were to be borne. Otherwise there might be food queues, riots and worse. In 1917 food riots sparked the Russian Revolution, brought down the Tsarist regime and took Russia out of the war. The government could not afford for that to happen in Britain. It became increasingly clear that the war front could not succeed without a sustainable home front.

The challenge was to create and maintain a home front in the neighbourhoods, workplaces and homes of Britain when faced with a significant proportion of men of working-age volunteering and later being conscripted into the Army and thus disappearing from the workforce. Staffordshire may be a little-studied county far away from London and the sea, but its diversity reminds us of the range of experiences to be found on the home front. At the time of the First World War, Staffordshire was bigger than it now is and included Wolverhampton and Walsall and much of the Black Country. The county ranged from highly urbanised areas, like the Potteries, manufacturing towns such as Leek or Burton-on-Trent, smaller towns such as Stone or Rugeley, as well as villages and smaller settlements scattered through a rural landscape. No industry dominated the county, although agriculture (mainly dairy) was as important as mining, ceramics, brewing, leather and various kinds of engineering. Sitting at the heart of England and Wales, Staffordshire was also traversed by the major communication networks of railways, roads and canals. This was important on the home front as the war prompted significant levels of mobility with men and women travelling to meet the demands of the war, whether as troops or as war workers. Nor did the war put an end to journeys by Staffordshire people: voluntarily for holidays, to visit family and for education and training, or the forced relocation of those who were interned as aliens or imprisoned as conscientious objectors. There were also new additions to the local home front, some more welcome than others: Belgian refugees, New Zealand troops and German prisoners of war. As a result many people passed through wartime Staffordshire, with some staying for the duration while others only paused at a railway buffet as their train speeded through England. Therefore, Staffordshire was diverse in terms of the type of settlements, the various local economies and the mix of people (part of long-standing communities or more recent arrivals). This means that exploring the home front, as created and lived in Staffordshire, offers an opportunity to examine not only how a local home front worked but the effect it had on daily life. In short, was everyone's experience the same and how did these experiences change over the duration of the war?

The richness of the material collected during the Appeals project means that only some of what we, the volunteers and I, uncovered has made it into this book, but what you will find within these covers reflects the wider evidence. This book weaves together the voices of people at the time from a range of material to create a picture of life on the Staffordshire home front, revealing how it varied and changed over the war. We wanted to show that it was possible to open up a window onto daily life on a local home front and to widen our understanding of what the First World War meant to ordinary people in provincial Britain whose experiences are too often overlooked. There is much more to tell of life on the Staffordshire home front: this is only a beginning.

CHAPTER ONE

WAR COMES TO STAFFORDSHIRE

In the early days of August 1914, most Staffordshire people of all ages and classes were focusing on their holidays rather than on distant events in continental Europe. Very few anticipated what would soon become known as the Great War and the ways in which the emergency would stretch out and gradually encroach upon every aspect of their daily lives. This new kind of warfare demanded a home front as well as a war front and would involve, in one way or another, women as well as men, the young and the old, and from the wealthiest to the poorest wherever they lived – in cities, suburbs, market towns, villages or deep in the countryside. Experiences were to be extraordinarily varied but few would not be challenged by the war years.

Yet in contemporary documents, from local council minutes or school log books to diaries and letters, the outbreak of the war is often barely acknowledged. Edith Birchall, a twenty-year-old from Tunstall, working as an uncertificated teacher, kept a diary through the war years. As the country drifted towards war, she was preparing to go to college in London to train as a teacher. On 31 July, Edith and her family left the Potteries to begin their journey to Ilfracombe, yet nowhere on their week's holiday does this observant diarist notice war preparations. On her return home on 7 August, three days after the outbreak of war, she commented: 'Note. The terrible European war has just begun. Belgians have so far held out splendidly against Germans'. After that there are no further references to the war until 25 October when she had left Staffordshire to begin college life in London. On that Sunday she noted, 'Many trains passed laden with men, cannons and horses'.[1]

In contrast, the outbreak of the war is much more evident in the letters between the children of J. C. Wedgwood, Radical Liberal MP for Newcastle-under-Lyme. Although home for their father was often London as he attended to his business in the House of Commons, his seven children (aged five to nineteen at the outbreak of war) were based at the family home of The Ark, Moddershall Oaks, Stone, in an area where many other members of the Wedgwood pottery dynasty also lived. Particularly after the estrangement of their parents – their mother, unusually for the time, left the family in 1913 – letters were an important way in which the family, especially the older children, kept in touch with one another and with their often absent father. By 3 September 1914, their father wrote urging Charles to join the 5th North Staffordshire Regiment by going to see Uncle Frank (Francis Hamilton Wedgwood, 1867–1930), who was a local recruiting officer. He explained to his daughter, 'He will be taught to shoot and that is the vital thing just now; for soon the Zeppelins will be over him and the fleet is none too safe from them, and then all men will be wanted. It won't do for Charles to funk; and you mustn't let him.'[2] Soon Charles was writing to his younger brother Josiah about his experiences with the reserves at Butterton Hall. This unoccupied large house in parkland had been quickly requisitioned by the military and Charles described the strenuous drilling, 14-mile route marches as well as outings to Newcastle swimming baths. Meanwhile their sister Rosamund, aged seventeen, was responsible for managing the family's finances, hosting Belgian refugees and reassuring her father that her younger sisters, 'the babies', were well. He in turn wrote to the children about his preparations to leave for Flanders leading

MR. WEDGWOOD, M.P., WOUNDED.

MR. JOSIAH WEDGWOOD, M.P.

Above left: Edith Birchall, aged twenty-one (private collection).

Above right: J. C. Wedgwood MP, from *Staffordshire Advertiser*, 15 May 1915.

an armoured column. For this branch of the Wedgwood family, the war arrived quickly in their daily lives. This was despite the fact that none of the males were of military age at the outbreak of war; the boys were too young and their father at forty-two would initially have been considered too old. However, he was a veteran of the South African war and soon became a Lieutenant-Commander in the Royal Naval Volunteer Reserve. All the males in this family would end up serving in the military, although two of the sisters were critical of the war, working with the No Conscription Fellowship. However, in August 1914, no one knew what this new war would mean for them.

In other households in Staffordshire the war came more unevenly into their lives. The weekend before war was declared a bank holiday, followed in a number of places by a Wakes Week. Looking back at the week in which war was declared (Tuesday 4 August), it is clear that the first way in which war came into the lives of many Staffordshire people was through the effect that mobilisation had on train services, upsetting many holiday plans. The *Staffordshire Advertiser*'s leader that week included the headline 'Spoilt Holidays':

Though a matter of small amount in comparison with the tremendous issues at stake, in a domestic sense we have to lament spoilt holidays for thousands of the population. And in these days of high pressure on the mental worker and of speeding up in manual labour, the loss of the annual holiday will be keenly felt.[3]

Many holiday events went ahead, including Stoke Wakes with its pleasure fair in Hanley: 'The young people have enjoyed themselves much as usual, hardly realizing the serious position in which their country is now placed'. This was the weekend where much had been planned. Agricultural and horticultural shows were regularly held on the holiday weekend. So it was in 1914: Keele Agricultural Show was 'marred by weather and war'. Other events were cancelled, from the Uttoxeter Agricultural Show to the garden party of Eccleshall's Unionist Association. This was also the time when boy scouts went away on camp: around seventy Walsall scouts were encamped on Cannock Chase while a Tunstall troop had been camping much further afield, near Brussels. More rural parts of the county had expected visitors and the business that came with them. In Great Haywood, far fewer visitors were noted than in years past because of the absence of excursion trains.

The scouts were not the only groups who seized the opportunity of a holiday weekend to go on camp: many of the local volunteers were away from home when the call came to muster. The Staffordshire Territorials were at St Asaph in North Wales. In the small hours of Monday, orders were given to each commanding officer to prepare to leave camp as soon as possible, although this was hampered by the seriously disrupted train service. Others were also trying to get back to Staffordshire. Under a headline 'Unpleasant Experiences on the Continent. Stafford Lady and Gentleman stranded in Paris', the story was told of a couple trying to return home from Switzerland who were frequently turned out of trains on their way as the whole continent seemed to be mobilising. Stranded in Paris, they found British banknotes were not accepted and that there was no food to be had. They had an early experience of what was to come – the queue. There was a 300-yard queue five abreast waiting for the railway booking office to open and a six-hour queue to get on the platform. In the end they

Some of the Uttoxeter Volunteers.

had to leave their luggage behind. The atmosphere in Stafford on their return was no less unusual, with people on the move and crowds milling about.

Stafford was described in the opening days of the war as like a garrison town, although it was Burton-on-Trent where the Staffordshire Reservists who had been called up were to be concentrated. They were initially called to local centres such as Lichfield and Hednesford. Many reservists resident in Staffordshire were part of regiments or the naval reserve located outside the county and they joined those seeking to travel on crowded trains. As the reservists left, 'Many pathetic farewell scenes were witnessed'. This sounds a little different to the 'enthusiastic scenes' reported in Newcastle on the Wednesday afternoon and evening. In the afternoon there were crowds in the vicinity of the barracks singing patriotic songs and cheering. In the evening khaki-clad territorials were to be seen in the streets and 'an occasional cheer gave an indication of the pent-up enthusiasm of the people'. Over a few days, a large number of men found themselves going on unplanned journeys while many more looked on. In Stafford, extraordinary crowds in the streets discussed news of the European war but there was also 'the desire for amusement, even in the midst of gravity'. Large houses gathered at the Picture Palace to be entertained but also to see the newsreels that included a view of the Staffordshire Infantry Territorials drilling on the Grammar School Field. This was a canny move by the theatre but it also anticipated the importance that news would have in this war, as well as meeting the desire to catch a glimpse of menfolk who had 'gone' into the forces.

The gathering together of the men who would make up the first British Expeditionary Force required speedy organisation within towns and cities across provincial England. Staffordshire,

A match undisturbed by the outbreak of war: Leek Cricket Club.

in the middle of the country, saw a considerable movement of men just in those first few days of the war both within the county and also across it as an army started to be assembled. In Leek, a large number of reservists left in such haste that at least two cricket matches had to be postponed. Practical arrangements had to be made swiftly including the commandeering of suitable horses. On Thursday afternoon the advance party of Leek reservists travelled to Stoke by train, and from there to Burton. The rest were expected to join them the following week, marching across the county from Leek via Ashbourne. Meanwhile accommodation had to be found in Burton for the 6,000 soldiers assembling there from across Staffordshire. All of this activity drew the crowds, particularly as most workplaces were shut.

The curious could be drawn to speakers who might provide some explanation of what was happening. A 'War Protest Meeting' on the evening of 4 August in St John's Square, Burslem, was addressed by the pacifist R. L. Outhwaite (1868–1930), Radical Liberal MP for Hanley. It attracted 1,500 people. His speech was constantly interrupted, which suggests that not all of those present shared Outhwaite's convictions or his analysis of how the country had found itself in such a perilous state. However, his speech was reported in detail in the local press, indicating it was still possible to provide other forms of argument that would soon be muted and even silenced. His tone was one of sorrow rather than anger. He provided a different narrative of what war would mean for the Potteries. This was not the language of the recruiter. He said,

The men they were at war with were their best customers, and when they were at war those men could buy no goods; therefore the men who manufactured the goods must inevitably join the ranks of the unemployed. ... The tragedy of war will fall upon the humble homes, the tragedy of war will fall upon the brave lads – I care none whether they be Englishmen, Germans or Russians – who have no enmity in their hearts. My sympathy goes out to them, because upon them fall the tragedy and horrors of war – not upon the great men who make wars for their own interests. ... Be as patriotic as you may, but let your patriotism concern itself also with the home that is made desolate because of war, the home in which starvation enters because of war.

He said he did not care if they never voted for him again, but he felt he had to tell the truth as he saw it. He asked for their help to 'mitigate as far as can be the sorrows, the widespread miseries that will fall upon the people of this country'. Here, the crowd broke out into applause. No resolution was submitted at the end of the meeting, for this was not really a protest but more a different vision of what war would mean for the men, women and children who would remain in Staffordshire while a war was fought far away. They were to be part of a new battleground – the home front – for which no significant preparations had been made. In those first days of war few could imagine what the First World War would mean for civilians and how long the war would go on. Yet a close reading of the first local newspapers of the war shows that many of the themes of the home front were already apparent.

As striking as the milling crowds, the families deprived of their holidays and those seeking news, distraction and even entertainment, are two other things: that for many life went on as usual and that when the war began to encroach on their lives it was not through the sound of marching men but through the disruptive effects of mobilisation on local economies. In the Cannock area, it was noted that 100 reservists had been called up and that these departures

had a considerable effect on public and private business establishments, though curiously enough the local police force embraced no reservists. Three men at the Hednesford post office and one at Cannock ... were affected whilst at Cannock Workhouse the Guardians were deprived of the services of the assistant Master, porter, and plumber ... The management of Cannock Hippodrome also lost the services of five of its employees who were recalled to their regiment.[4]

In the first week of the war there were meetings across the county to try to anticipate what the economic effect of war would be on local communities. When the Staffordshire Territorial Force Association met in Stafford on Wednesday afternoon (5 August), their principal focus was on recruiting but they also discussed how to ensure the families of soldiers and sailors were looked after. The Soldiers' and Sailors' Families Association (SSFA) was to swing into action in each district, learning the lessons of the Boer War to make sure that there was no overlap between relief organisations and that everyone pursued a uniform practice across the

Portrait of Baron Charnwood, 1919.

country. The local aristocracy and gentry were very much to the fore in the leadership of these sorts of organisations. So it was Lord Charnwood (1864–1945) – a former Liberal MP and a Mayor of Lichfield (1909–11) – who reflected to the meeting on the expected economic effects of war. He did not anticipate that trades generally would suffer but as some would, a plan was needed to meet distress when it arose. There was more than a little noblesse oblige about this but also a more pragmatic recognition that economic hardship might inhibit volunteers who would prioritise the welfare of their families over the patriotic call to the Colours.

In those early days, not everyone was as sanguine about the economic costs that war would have on Staffordshire. In the Potteries it was reported that there was 'an anxious feeling as to the prospects of trade'. All the factories were closed for the holidays and it was thought that there was little probability of work being resumed at the end of the holiday week. It was said that 'with no work, there are no wages coming in, and the want of cash, combined with the rise in the price of food, must give rise to grave anxiety'. It was in this context that Wedgwood & Sons, one of the leading pottery firms of the area, let it be known, 'Largely with a view of checking panic, we shall open for work as usual after the holidays and thereafter only gradually close if absolutely necessary.' As people locally would have understood, one of the issues was predicting the effect on such an export-driven industry of the loss of markets due to hostilities. It was, therefore, pointed out in the local press that the markets of the America, Australia and New Zealand remained open to the industry while Germany and France only absorbed a fraction of the products usually exported from the Potteries. In Stafford, attempts were made to allay fears of economic disruption. It was announced that the local boot and shoe factories and the engineering factory Siemens would reopen on Monday after the week's holiday.

Siemens had additional challenges. Siemens' workers were offered the reassurance that although a great deal of material used by the firm came from Germany, arrangements could be made to make the parts required at Stafford. Perhaps more unsettling, and prefiguring another theme of the war years, was that the manager of the works, E. O. Kieffer, was a lieutenant in the German Army. He had already left the country together with other members of the Siemens' staff for service with the Kaiser's forces. This clearly caused anxieties among the Stafford workforce as not only was the company's patriotism called into question, the absence of key members of staff could affect the ability of the business to respond effectively to as yet unknown demands of a war economy. Concerned at what they saw as malicious attacks on their employer and therefore their livelihoods, workers' representatives at Siemens wrote a letter to *The Daily Telegraph* explaining,

Messrs. Siemens, although bearing a German name, have displayed more patriotism towards England than many firms who claim to be absolutely British. We also wish to state that in normal times about 2,000 workpeople are employed at these Stafford works, of which approximately 4 per cent are foreigners, comprising Germans, who have grown grey in the service of the firm, others born in England, and a good number of other nationalities, not alien enemies.

It has also been stated in reference to Siemens that Germany benefits to the extent of £35,000 annually in profits, without any corresponding advantage to this country. Seeing that the company pay quite £100,000 per annum in wages at their Stafford works alone, is this not a decided counter advantage?[5]

Here we learn not only the size and value of the Siemens business to the local economy of Stafford but also the kind of criticisms that could destabilise a company (its patriotic duty to surrender its share of workers to the military as well as the easy slide from a German name to assumed support for the enemy). It was in the workers' as well as the owner's interests to set the record straight, but choosing to do so in a national newspaper reveals how dangerous these slurs could be to the wellbeing of Stafford workers and their families in the new context of war. Local Stafford employers like Siemens were operating in a local, national and international economy, all of which were going to be dislocated by the war but in ways which were not predictable in August 1914. The same was the case, in slightly different ways, for other industries in the county.

For the Staffordshire working class – the majority of the local population – the onset of war and the move to a domestic home front brought particular worries. The first wartime edition of *The Wolverhampton Worker* stressed the patriotic example that the trade union movement would give, but also expressed anxiety about the effect of war on the livelihoods of local workers' families. They warned of the threat to hours and wages that the war might prompt, particularly the danger of high levels of unemployment. Unions were urged to prevent the working of overtime in occupations where members were already unemployed and to share-out work in order to minimise the risk of more unemployment.[6] This was the kind of distress, as it was termed, that many in Staffordshire feared. Existing organisations were therefore reactivated and new ones started. The relieving of distress caused by the war was to be a recurring theme throughout the long years of the home front.

With no welfare state yet, economic distress could only be relieved by the poor law operated through the Boards of Guardians, charities and the combination of workers to protect wage rates and jobs through trade unions. The first two were ubiquitous, while the latter was a growing movement that was to emerge strengthened from its wartime experience, but whose coverage of industries and of types of workers (particularly the unskilled and women) was patchy. In the first week of the war there is evidence of all three mechanisms at work, but the emergency prompted the establishment of a new fund through which all civilian distress was to be dealt with and which would form the focus of all donations so as not to dissipate energies. The first wartime edition of the *Staffordshire Advertiser* already carried a notice from the Borough of Stafford National Relief Fund, a local branch of the fund inaugurated by the Prince of Wales for 'relief of distress which may occur amongst the people of the country in consequence of the war'. People were asked to give generously in envelopes addressed to the Prince of Wales, Buckingham Palace, via Stafford's Mayor. Regular reports on the operation of the various local versions of this fund and its supporting Citizen Committees as well as criticisms of the adequacy and accessibility of these funds to Staffordshire's needy, were to be common themes across the war, as were concerns about the make-up of the local committees who distributed these funds. What is clear is that from the outset there was recognition locally that the war might cause hardship, particularly to women and children, whether because of absent breadwinners or short time or unemployment as industries shifted to a wartime economy.

This was not just an urban phenomenon. Agriculture was an important part of the Staffordshire economy and was to become a crucial element in sustaining the new home front. In the first days of the war, the agricultural pages of the local press made little reference to the emergency. Seighford, a small village to the west of Stafford, reported in detail on the state of its crops, including 'Potatoes promise capitally, but the wet weather has affected them and some are going bad. Sun is badly wanted'. Fruit was said to be fairly plentiful, especially damsons in certain localities. Weather rather than war was the concern. Yet in the next column the latest news from the markets across the country showed a rather different picture: in many places there was little or no business and there were warnings against panic. Farmers and millers were thought to be holding back corn from the markets while wheat shipments from America and Canada were awaited. At nearby Derby Corn Market, it was reported that on Friday 7 August, 'The market was at a complete standstill today. There was nothing doing and prices were simply unobtainable.' Farmers were advised by the Board of Agriculture not to slaughter stock, particularly breeding stock, despite the current high prices they could get for meat and the feared future costs of feeding stuffs. They could not know that this short termism was to occur in Germany when the economic blockade began to bite, exacerbating tensions between rural and urban communities who each thought the other was benefiting from their hardship. Agriculture as an industry and the tensions between

Learning to contribute to food production: a boy's gardening class, Seighford County School, 1912.

large farmers, tenant – farmers and smallholders, and agricultural labourers were to figure as a significant issue on the British home front, including in Staffordshire. Increasingly pressing was the role of agriculture in calculations about where manpower was needed between the war and the home front, and then what part of the home front. For Staffordshire this was to be an important way in which the war would be experienced because it was a county where no industry dominated. As the first days of the war showed, food was going to be a crucial factor in the survival of the British home front, in Staffordshire as elsewhere.

Reports across the county describing the local effects of the outbreak of war all comment on increases in food prices and on panic buying. At a special meeting of Stafford Town Council convened by the mayor, there were two topics: regulating the food supply and the unpatriotic wealthy. The mayor felt that they needed to prevent people laying in large amounts of provisions and thereby pushing up prices. This was urgent

in view of what certain of the wealthier people have already done in the way of getting in extensive quantities of goods. ... Prices of foodstuffs have already advanced to a considerable extent, and it is largely the result of a rush to secure unlimited supplies of provisions.

The meeting exhorted the people of Stafford not to purchase more than their usual weekly supply of provisions and asked tradesmen to agree to limit their sales to the usual quantities bought by customers. In the council's discussion of what was already termed 'the food question', the mayor called for cooperation between tradesmen and shoppers; another councillor (a local employer) agreed that something must be done but insisted it should be voluntary; while a Labour councillor emphasised their duty to safeguard the welfare of women and children and suggested 'a committee of public safety', with its revolutionary overtones.

Another councillor thought that it is was not surprising that people had responded as they had: 'They must remember that no living man had gone through a time like the present'. The president of the local Cooperative Society also explained how it had responded: urging their members to practice the strictest economy; only supplying the normal requirements of members; asking members to stick to the store they normally patronised; and making every effort to keep prices down. Others talked of 'panic-stricken people' and the 'selfishness of some of the richer people'. All of these often contradictory ideas on how to solve a problem that they all recognised prefigure a range of attempts that were taken locally to deal with what eventually became a food crisis. Although at this point leading figures in Stafford hoped that this particular calamity would soon pass, they nevertheless passed a resolution calling on the government to control and regulate the food supply of the country during the emergency.

In contrast it was said in the Potteries that although the price of foodstuffs had gone up as elsewhere, 'no great alarm is felt on the score of scarcity'. In Stafford some grocers and provision shops closed their doors at midday Wednesday because of such a great demand for goods. To add to the uncertainty, local banks, which had been shut because of the bank holiday, had then remained closed until the following Friday. In an attempt to control prices, the government urged that maximum retail prices should be agreed for staple foods and the local press printed a list of prices so that ordinary shoppers could have a sense of what was considered a fair price. However, in the first days of the war, it was reported that in Burton-on-Trent sugar was double its normal price and a loaf of bread had gone up a halfpenny and, more worrying for the local industry, malting barley was practically unobtainable and one large firm had had to close down. In Wolverhampton, people were reported as leaving shops without making purchases when they were faced with price increases. There was also a reported shortage of cash and thus a novel action was described – paying by cheque in excess of what was required and being given the balance in change: cash-back!

Bread was a particular concern because of the country's heavy reliance on imported wheat and because it was fundamental to the working-class diet. A Stafford miller said, 'We do not see any cause at all for any panic as far as food supplies are concerned. There is enough stock in the country to last six months, and judging by today's market prices, there is no necessity at present to give more than 40 shillings a sack for best flour.' The North Staffordshire Bakers Association decided to make no increase in the price of bread before Monday 10 August, not yet a week after the outbreak of war. But in Walsall the bakers decided to increase the price of a 4-lb loaf by a halfpenny. What was clear was that neither the experience of shoppers nor local responses by shopkeepers was uniform across the county. Yet the feeling remained that because of the war prices had been unnecessarily raised and scarcities created by the selfish acts of the few and that it would be the poor who would be hardest hit. The *Staffordshire Advertiser* reprinted *The Times*'s call for 'the confiscation of unnecessary accumulations', which foreshadowed later action against food hoarders. But this intervention would only become a realistic possibility later in the war.

In the first wartime edition of the *Staffordshire Advertiser*, it is striking that many of the issues that would become central to the experience of people on the home front as the war stretched out were already being aired. How would people survive? What would be the economic cost of the war? How would the families of soldiers and sailors manage in the absence of the breadwinner? What would happen to local industry and jobs? Would there be an equality of sacrifice or would having sufficient money cushion an individual or family from the privations suffered by others? Whether or not individual Staffordshire men and women actively supported the war in August 1914, or saw it as something they could do little about, all would find that it would gradually seep into the routines of daily life as living on a home front became a reality.

CHAPTER TWO

CREATING A HOME FRONT

The challenge for the county once war was declared was not only to provide men for the Army but also to organise the new home front. This was new for everyone. Infrastructure was needed to support the military campaign while local industry and agriculture had to move onto a war footing. All of these tasks were linked together as every man who enlisted left a gap in the workforce and in the economic support of a particular family or household. While this was thought to be a short-term crisis, the dislocation of civilian life could be tolerated, but increasingly it became clear that this war would not be 'over by Christmas'. Far away from the sound of the guns, a provincial county had to adapt to its new circumstances, changing expectations and even behaviour as the reality of living on the home front began to impinge on daily life.

Soon it became evident that organising military recruitment on such an unprecedented scale required more than the beating of a patriotic drum. Volunteers wanted reassurance that their jobs would be there for them on their return and that their families would be able to manage without their wages. The balance between the exhortation that it was the duty of young men, particularly single men, to volunteer and the removal of the economic disincentive to enlist, was to shift once the patriotic euphoria (for some, at least) began to wane. Right from the outset local Staffordshire firms made clear the arrangements they would make for employees who volunteered. In August 1914 in Stafford, Siemens announced they would pay full wages to their workers who enlisted while Bostocks offered to pay two-thirds of each employee's earnings. At the same time it was also thought necessary to set up a Stafford branch of the Soldiers' and Sailors' Families Association to relieve distressed dependents of those who volunteered. This committee began its work within days of the outbreak of war.

Across the autumn large enlistment events were held in major halls and market squares across the county. Borough Hall, Stafford, had never held so many people when a recruitment meeting was held in October, addressed by Lord Charles Beresford (1846–1919) – popularly known as the 'member for the navy'. He made much of the dangers of alien enemy spies and as a result there was a good response to the call for recruits with Beresford shaking the hand of each volunteer. However set-piece meetings did not produce the volume of recruits that the Army required and soon the tone of reports on local recruiting campaigns changed. Now men would be disgraced or even threatened into volunteering, as at this meeting in Fazeley:

It was a disgrace to the village that so many young men were absent. They did not know whether it was ignorance, or indifference, or cold feet. The nation was at stake, and it was their absolute and bounden duty to enlist. Unless the young men of the country came forward voluntarily, the Militia Act might be brought into operation, and the young men would have to go. Men with eight or nine children volunteered and joined the Colours, leaving good jobs, and the young men should not have allowed that to have been possible.[1]

FOR KING AND COUNTRY.

WELL DONE, NORTH STAFFORDS!

SEVENTH and EIGHTH NEW BATTALIONS
Now Full Up.

THIRD and FOURTH NORTH STAFFORDS
Made up to 2,000 Strong.

500 RECRUITS AT DEPOT.

NORTH STAFFORD MEN STILL WANTED

To Form 9th and 10th BATTALIONS.

Recruits now Enlisted Serve One Day with the Colours and Remainder with Army Reserve, at 6d. a-Day until such time as called upon by Army Council.

EX-N.C.O.'s up to 45 WANTED.
EX-COLOUR-SERGEANTS up to 50.

'North Stafford Men Still Wanted', from *Staffordshire Advertiser*, 12 September 1914.

Local recruiting committees were formed to ensure more forensic sweeps were made in neighbourhoods to locate eligible men, principally single men between eighteen and forty. Evidence was to be collected of the names, addresses, dependents and occupations of these men together with details of local retired army men, married men capable of joining up and men with any military experience. So began what would continue to be various attempts to record an accurate picture of the nation's manpower and potential military power. Once identified these men (collectively and individually) would be subject to persuasion through public meetings, posters and through the attention of women workers, who would visit mothers and wives during the afternoon. Women were quickly recognised as a useful source of psychological pressure on their men. At a recruitment meeting held in Tamworth in November it was urged from the platform that local women should 'encourage the men to join the Army and not hang back; let them follow the path that leads to honour and self-respect'. Like many other enlistment meetings, a wounded soldier spoke to the crowd. Sergeant Godderidge, wounded at Mons, urged men to volunteer 'before it was finished'. He said he had four brothers and two brothers-in-law at the front. And most tellingly he said, 'He left a wife and three children behind, and they were being well looked after. There was nothing to hold a man back but himself.'[2]

Many men on the home front were swept up into the committees, meetings and bureaucracy that constituted recruitment in the early months of the war. One was Albert Blizzard (1862–1949), brick and tile manufacturer of Congleton, who was chairman and managing director of Messrs George Woolliscroft & Sons, Hanley. The company had three factories in the Potteries. Blizzard was part of the local elite who together formed networks that were to be crucial in creating Staffordshire's home front. Known to be 'Energetic and enterprising by nature' and with a long history of involvement in the Volunteers, Blizzard was typical of the new breed of recruiters. A major at the outbreak of war, he was promoted in January 1915 to lieutenant-colonel. Col Blizzard quickly became a familiar figure within the local press and in the towns and villages of the county as he orchestrated what often appeared to be a personal campaign. Soon he even had a song written in his honour, 'Blizzard's Bold Brigade', which was dedicated to the 5th North Staffordshire Regiment. Copies were sold for a shilling with the proceeds going to fund comforts for the men of the regiment.[3]

Although Blizzard had hoped to go to France, instead he used his formidable skills in Staffordshire. Before the first year of the war was over, he had raised a full battalion and trained them for nearly six months. There was a strong personal identification between him and 'his men'. He later recalled, 'In the numerous hard fought actions in which the Battalions took part I always lost a number of good friends and gallant comrades and each loss increased the sense of loneliness one cannot help to feel under such circumstances, though there is so much to do that one has fortunately little time for thought.'[4]

Recruiters like Blizzard faced particular local challenges. By the end of February 1915 28,400 Staffordshire men 'had gone' – the phrase increasingly used – to the Colours or, to put it another way, were no longer in the local workforce. Within districts there were considerable variations, and scapegoats were sought for the shortfall. Some suggested that rural areas had not responded sufficiently to the call while others felt that miners were holding back. At the Newcastle recruiting committee, these views were aired along with the example of a little village where it was said eighty-one men were eligible but would not enlist 'unless they were fetched' – an increasingly popular phrase on the lips of recruiters. To encourage more volunteers the criteria for what made a recruit kept changing: in February 1915 an improvement in recruiting was seen in Stafford, not unconnected with new War Office guidelines that regiments could now accept men who were only 5 feet 1 inch tall, provided that they were aged nineteen to thirty-eight and had a chest size of 34 inches.[5]

It was this state of affairs in Staffordshire that led to increasing energy being given to drives to increase not only the quantity but also the type of recruits. It was felt that there were too many married and older men among the volunteers. After eight months of war, it was reported that in North Staffordshire over 70 per cent of men of military age had not enlisted. The issue was how to persuade them to volunteer, as the Staffordshire recruiters would not countenance conscription. The Stoke Recruitment Committee undertook a local canvas and found that it was the youths in clerkships rather than manual occupations who were not enlisting.[6]

Col Blizzard spent much of the early summer of 1915 leading recruitment campaigns around the highways of Staffordshire, particularly in the smaller villages where it was thought

MAJOR A. E. BLIZZARD.
(*5th North Staffordshire Regiment.*)
Managing Director of Messrs. Geo. Woolliscroft and Son,
Ltd., of Hanley, who has volunteered for the front.

Major A. E. Blizzard, 1914.

The cover of the song 'Blizzard's Bold Brigade'.

men were not volunteering with sufficient eagerness. On Saturdays after men had finished work they might be drawn to the spectacle of Blizzard's battalion route marching through the neighbourhood, led by Blizzard on horseback followed by a band and with set-piece meetings organised at stages through the day. To draw the crowds, Blizzard ensured that the local 'great and the good' turned out to greet the soldiers and to exhort local volunteers, often from their tenants or workforce. In Audley, the local squire Reginald Wood (1842–1924) of Bignall End Hall was the focus for the recruitment meeting. He produced a star attraction for the soldiers – his son-in-law Sir Frederick Bridge(1844–1924). Bridge was a well-known composer. His task at Audley was to provide the accompaniment to a new patriotic song he had written. This was only the second time that it had been heard in public. Sir Frederick told the crowd, 'I played it to the King last week; today I am playing it to the colliers.' The route of this march went through a landscape crowded with pits as the 650 men on parade marched through Knutton, Alsagers Bank, Halmer End and Miles Green to Audley – with crowds all the way.[7]

Crucial to this and other recruiting rallies held across North Staffordshire that summer was the presence of Blizzard himself. At each meeting he addressed the crowd. At Audley he said he wanted 550 men, even though the community had already sent 270 to the Colours. His words suggested why vigorous recruitment in Staffordshire remained a priority:

Perhaps the only reason which kept men back was that they did not realise the imminence of the danger to this country. If the fighting were at Wolstanton, there was not a man present who would not be in it … If they had any blood in them, the young men would come out at once and show their womankind and especially their sweethearts, that they were ready to defend their homes.

However, the response was often muted: 'outside the towns one noted the fewness of young men about. They were practically all elderly people and children who cheered the battalion as they went by'. At Eccleshall, the town was 'beflagged' with smartly dressed Red Cross ladies and gentlemen standing by stalls covered with tea and pies for the soldiers. The crowd was told that although 200 local men had enlisted, 'although it was good, it was not sufficient'. From the platform, Lord Stafford (1864–1941) – soon to be the country's

The platform at the recruiting parade at Audley, from *Staffordshire Weekly Sentinel*, 8 May 1915.

Director of Mines and Torpedoes – thanked Blizzard but then turned on women: some women were magnificent but 'in his wandering recruiting he found many women who were against the war, and who refused to let their sons and brothers go … He hoped the women would do their best to make their men-folk go, and tell them what their duty was'. He said many shops in the district employed young able-bodied men to do work that women could do equally well. He was certain there were young women and girls who were prepared to take on this work while the men were doing their duty elsewhere.[8] One man's decision to volunteer could have significant repercussions not just for himself and his family but also for the home front he would be leaving.

In the period before the introduction of conscription in 1916, Blizzard was a successful recruiter and trainer for the North Staffordshire regiments: no fewer than 17,000 Staffordshire men were said to have passed through his hands.[9] He continued to be a familiar figure in the local press, congratulated for his achievements at the time and remembered with affection after the war. His work, like that of other recruiters, not only was crucial to the war front but helped to shape the local home front.

Creating the Military Camps in Staffordshire

Placing the county on a war footing in this new kind of warfare was never just about finding sufficient men for the armed services. A home front had to be created that would meet the unanticipated demands of sustaining the war front and the civilian population at a time of economic blockade and with increasing numbers of men missing from the workforce. One way in which Staffordshire moved onto a war footing was to provide the necessary infrastructure to make war on this scale, in this case by constructing and then sustaining the military camps at Brocton on Cannock Chase. All the facilities were required to accommodate, feed, clothe, occupy and train local, national and international troops (this was to become the base for many soldiers from New Zealand) as well as prisoners of war, together with the means to move the men, their equipment and all the support services on and off the camp. This was a large task for which no plans had been made. The work was undertaken by civilian contractors organised through the local Rural District Council (RDC) to meet the specifications of the military authorities. The sourcing of sufficient labourers, equipment and materials needed to create what was in effect a new town provided unforeseen challenges for this part of Staffordshire and new problems and benefits for local communities.

Work did not begin on Brocton camp until 1915. Road and rail links had to be constructed, which required the recruitment of a sizeable workforce when many men were already either in the Army or in war work. People and machinery were advertised for within and beyond Staffordshire. In April 1915 the *Birmingham Daily Post* carried adverts placed by a local contractor at the camp. They wanted to hire, 'for three months certain', motor lorries and light tractors to work on good roads from station to camp for seven days a week. They also advertised separately for two different categories of workers for the military camp in course of erection: two competent builder's clerks and one junior, as well as a lady shorthand typist and a lady clerk used to the building trade.[10] These suggest the scale of the project and the range of skills required to execute the War Office's plan.

The labour drawn to Brocton had to be housed as most came from outside the area. They also had to be fed and entertained or occupied when not working. All of this had practical consequences for local people. Soon the presence of large numbers of labourers started to intrude into the local press, particularly through cases at the police court. Workers from the camp were now regularly charged with being drunk and disorderly. Some had come a considerable distance to work at Brocton, such as David Nicholl, a native of Glasgow who

MEN ARE STILL URGENTLY REQUIRED TO CARRY ON THE WAR.

THERE ARE VACANCIES FOR MEN IN

All Infantry Regiments ; Men used to horses as Drivers, Remount and Veterinary Duties ; Royal Horse and Royal Field Artillery ; Nottingham Gun and Ammunition Brigade ; Various Tradesmen and Clerks in Royal Engineers, Army Service Corps, and Army Ordnance ; and the Royal Army Medical Corps is again open for Eligible Men.

Motor Cycle Machine Gun Company are seeking good Men used to Motor Cycles.

Men for the Lincoln Regiment are specially called for.

Separation Allowances for Wives, Children, and Dependents on the new higher scale.

Any men not fit for service may assist their country with an Armament or Munition Firm by applying to the nearest Labour Exchange.

APPLY TO THE RECRUITING OFFICES AT

STAFFORD, BURTON-ON-TRENT, UTTOXETER, TAMWORTH, RUGELEY; or MAJOR T. PAMPLIN GREEN,

Headquarters 64th Recruiting Area, The Barracks, LICHFIELD.

A Railway Warrant will be sent on application to enable a man to attend at Headquarters for enlistment.

'Men are still urgently required', *Staffordshire Advertiser*, 8 May 1915.

admitted 'he had had a wee drap of Johnnie Walker and knew he was tight'. In response to this social problem, the police applied to Stafford licensing bench to curtail opening hours at local pubs. They were able to show that in comparison to before the war cases of drunkenness had nearly doubled in the first four months of 1915. The majority of the offenders were workers at Brocton camp. This was a problem for the nearby town of Stafford but also for the camp where it was reported that the workers 'are dilatory in their work owing to drunkenness overnight'. Earlier in the war, Stafford police had tried to get licensing hours reduced when there were 200 troops billeted in the town. By April 1915 when there were 600 labourers employed at Brocton, they felt the magistrates had to take action. Local publicans protested that it was unfair 'to put so grievous a burden on the shoulders of men who were as loyal as they were. They wanted "mutuality of sacrifice"'. Nevertheless, in May licensing hours were restricted for the eight pubs within the military area of the camp. They would have to close at 9 p.m. The colonel-in-charge anticipated that soon there would be a 1,000 men working on the Chase and thought such restrictions (he suggested that no drink should be served before 11 a.m. or after 8 p.m.) were 'very necessary'. Changing local licensing hours affected more than the workers at the camp. The licensees said that it would prevent agricultural labourers from getting their beer in the morning before going 3 or 4 miles into the country for work.[11]

The building of the camp led to business opportunities for many, whether in terms of wages, contracts or ancillary business, feeding and housing the waves of different workers who were required to build and then maintain the camp. In May 1915 it was announced that a site adjoining the Brocton camp had been secured by a London syndicate for the immediate erection of an up-to-date cinema, capable of seating a thousand. A company had been formed in which local citizens would take a prominent part. By November, troops had begun to arrive, presenting more business opportunities. Stafford Cooperative Society advertised teas at moderate charges to Brocton camp soldiers every Saturday at their Central Hall from 2.30 to 9 p.m.[12]

However, the building work was not complete. In December, pipe fitters were wanted to provide hot-and cold water for the camp. To aid hiring this new group of workmen, attention was drawn to a pay rate of 10½d an hour, with time and a half on Saturday afternoons and double time on Sundays. This suggests that men were relatively well paid but worked very long hours. Indeed, the rates of pay offered to workers at the camp had serious knock-on effects on the surrounding economy. Just the month before the Staffordshire Chamber of Agriculture had heard a different view of what a camp like Brocton meant for other local employers:

Those farmers who had the misfortune to live near a military camp had been hit a great deal harder than those whose farms were further away. It was difficult to keep men satisfied on £1 or 30s a week when they saw lads earning more in 2 or 3 days than farmers can afford to pay their labourers to work full time. All honour was due to these men who had resisted the temptation of higher wages, and the sneers and reproaches of their neighbours, and remained loyal to their farms.[13]

As the war continued there was increasing tension about the rates some workers could get undertaking work of national importance, particularly those paid 'war bonuses', as this could exacerbate the shortage of labour in other areas of the economy.

This huge project, prompted entirely by the war, was now moving into its next phase as a functioning military camp. Its impact on local communities continued to be significant as it offered business opportunities as well as employment both directly and indirectly in the surrounding villages and towns. By January 1916 the camp had a post office, an electric power station and a YMCA hut for the troops, as well as the barracks, canteens and kitchens that one would expect. Labourers from the camp were still appearing at

Women from the Army Catering Corps, Brocton camp, 1917.

the local police courts charged with drunkenness but in the courts as well as in the wider community the focus was now moving to the local effects of a new and larger population at the camps – soldiers. People in Stafford turned to ways to provide recreation for the large numbers of soldiers who came into the town on Sundays from the camp – teas and smoking rooms were the favoured options. Civilians continued to work at the camps. One example was a bricklayer at Brocton camp who was turned down for exemption from military service by Stafford Tribunal in March 1916 despite claiming to be the sole support of his elderly widowed mother. He earned a good wage of £3 in a full week. But when pressed by the military representative he admitted his mother also received some money from his sister who worked in a boot factory and from his soldier brother. The decision of the tribunal was that his mother would have to cope without her son's Brocton camp earnings and he must enter the Army. Other work was also available for civilians: 'WOMAN WANTED to Cook for a small Staff at Brocton Camp. – Apply, Leader, YMCA Hut, near Post Office'.[14]

The building of Brocton camp and the civilians who kept it working once the soldiers arrived are part of the story of how Staffordshire organised to put itself on a war footing. The construction of the camps on Cannock Chase showed businesses, local authorities and a local workforce adapting to new demands, particularly the consequences of importing labour into the area. The building of Brocton camp would not have happened but for the war. However, in the end, no aspect of industry or agriculture could escape from the new circumstances of an economy that had to arm and sustain the country as it discovered what 'total war' meant. How did that apply to Staffordshire?

Putting Industry and Agriculture on a War Footing

In the opening month of the war, there had been a sense of economic paralysis in some of the towns of Staffordshire. One example was Rugeley, which at the end of August 1914 was reported to be 'suffering considerably from the effects of War':

Local trade is at a very low ebb, and several large workshops have been forced to close down. There is likelihood, also, that the mines will be affected, but to what extent this will be so is not yet known. The railway service being hampered, the collieries are not able to get their coal away with any degree of facility, and there is a reported lack of timber, which is proving a handicap. At Armitage the Pottery Works have closed down with no immediate prospect of restarting.[15]

Yet in other ways, the war affected local industries and agriculture unevenly and sometimes surprisingly slowly.

In the first months of the war, local industry seemed to be more concerned about maintaining markets for their existing products rather than turning themselves over to producing new goods for the war. In Walsall it was feared that the prohibition of exports of saddlery and harnesses that could be used for military purposes would bring the ordinary export trade to a complete standstill: 'America would not be slow to capture the trade which we lost'.[16] In North Staffordshire, the ceramics industry wanted government support so that their pottery could compete with German goods in America.

Many worried about what was felt to be the continuing advantage that German products had in the wartime domestic market and the ill-effect this had on local businesses in Staffordshire. Various local Chambers of Commerce demanded that all German goods should be indelibly marked, 'Made in Germany', as 'Be Patriotic' and 'Support British Industries' labels had been spotted in shops on what was German pottery. It was suggested that some unscrupulous local manufacturers had imported goods from abroad, decorated them and then sold them as English goods: 'it showed that their enemies were not all outside this country'. Meanwhile business went on, so the Second Pottery and Glass Fair 'opened quietly' in February 1915 in Stoke-on-Trent. It ran for a week with fifty firms represented and buyers not just from Britain but also from Canada, the United States, South America and the Continent. It was said that 'it is fully expected that the local industry will receive and retain an important advantage from the fair being held at a time when the German output is paralysed, and when buyers in neutral countries are inquiring whether Staffordshire can supply what they have hitherto taken from Germany'.[17]

The effect of new government contracts for war materials gradually began to become evident across the county. Many peacetime products traditionally made in Staffordshire could be used to equip the armed services. Already in September 1914, John Shannon & Sons announced that they had secured several large contracts for the supply of clothing to British soldiers. This meant, they said, that they would be able to continue their factories at Tamworth and Walsall full time during the approaching winter. The *Tamworth Herald* noted that this was 'gratifying news to the people of Tamworth, and particularly the women workers, because but for these contracts there would inevitably have been a shortage of work for women at the factories'.[18] Shaws at Willenhall got their first government contracts for brass stirrups, bits and buckles in October 1914 while shoe factories in Stafford were also soon working to equip military forces.

What was termed 'the war rush' particularly made a difference to local businesses that had been depressed at the outbreak of war. The leather trades in Walsall, particularly saddlery and harness-making, were by 1915 working overtime: 'every man or woman who has any experience of the trade has been pressed into the service and very large wages are being earned'. They were not just making military leather ware, as the fancy leather goods market such as ladies handbags was also continuing as orders was being received that had formerly gone to Germany or Austria. The buoyancy of the leather goods industry was also noticed by its workforce. In April the workers demanded an increase in the rate of pay for cutters and dayworkers from 8s to 1s an hour with time and a half for overtime and double pay for Sunday work. The employers said this was unjustifiable, particularly as a large number of unskilled workers had been drawn into the trade as a result of big military contracts being placed in the town. From the workers' point of view, the issue was the effect of the increased cost of living that the war had created and their concern to reduce the number of casual dayworkers who could undercut established wage rates. No agreement was reached and the case was sent for arbitration to the new Trades Dispute Board. The war had brought new conditions, challenges and opportunities as well as new structures to try to deal with them.[19]

Munitions work also began in Staffordshire. The Turner Motor Manufacturing Co., Wolverhampton, had government contracts for lathes for making shells. Knutton Iron and Steel Co. prosecuted two of its workers for absenting themselves from employment when they should have been contributing to the company's efforts to complete contracts for minesweeping for the Admiralty. 'So urgent were the contracts that the Government had sent back to work four men who had enlisted.'[20] Increasingly the question was where the necessary workforce was to come from to meet the new demands of a war economy within different parts of Staffordshire. As we will see both boy and women's labour began to be considered as substitutes for missing male workers and to undertake new war work.

However, while some parts of the county's industries revived or were sustained through the need to equip the Army and Navy, the effects were not even. At the South Staffordshire Iron and Steel Market in October 1914 it was said, 'Firms who have Government contracts in hand are working night and day, but outside these particular lines there is not much doing'. Others worried about the effects of the war on local industry and agriculture. The Lichfield Chamber

Blacksmiths at Endon Smithy, with a huge pile of horseshoes produced for the war effort.

of Trade lamented the loss of so many employees who had joined the Army and the numbers of horses that had been commandeered. They 'hoped that the public would take into consideration the difficulties under which the traders now suffered, and make allowance for any shortcomings on their part'. By May 1915 they saw opportunities too: three military camps had been erected on the Heath, 'and no doubt a good deal of trade would be derived therefrom'.[21]

The Staffordshire Chamber of Agriculture also felt that war was affecting their 900-strong membership. At their annual meeting in February 1915 they underlined the contribution that agriculture was already making to the war effort. Their view was that 'the best form of patriotism that farmers can show is to get the utmost possible out of the land ... and stimulate larger production of agricultural wealth'. Interestingly, at this stage of the war their priority does not seem to have been food. In order to meet the actual and expected shortfall in agricultural labour they considered demanding that boys be permitted to leave school at twelve and, even, 'to take a leaf out of the books of France and Belgium, and first appeal to the women of the land'.[22]

Local farmers were conscious that they were beginning to get a bad press and protested against allegations that they were holding up supplies of wheat to the detriment of national interests or that they were responsible for its high price: 'it was deplorable that there should be a section of the community who seemed to have nothing to do but try and raise ill feeling against the farmers ... It was serious because it was playing the German's game'. By March 1915 the Chamber of Agriculture was raising an issue that would come to dominate manpower management in the county: they wanted a ruling from London 'whether the greater necessity was for more men or more food. They could not do two things at once with the same materials'.[23] Yet until the introduction of conscription in 1916 there was little guidance from central government on this important matter. Everything was left to the market. As a result each local economy had to deal alone with the effects of a diminishing workforce, the mobility of labour and the effects of competition from differing wage rates in a context of the rising cost of living. In addition, as well as beginning to turn over production to meet contracts generated through the War Office, most local economies tried at least in the opening years of the war to maintain the continuity of peacetime business as it was unclear how long the emergency would last.

It was not just employers who worried about these issues. There was also a sense that the community more generally had to prepare itself for new challenges. At the beginning of September 1914, the Walsall Workers War Emergency Committee (WWWEC) was formed to represent the interests of working people in the new wartime economy. The WWWEC said, 'They were going to see that their class, which had to do the bulk of the fighting, and were going to produce the materials for the army, the guns and the clothes – should be looked after.'[24] The committee consisted of trade unionists (mostly men) who wanted to ensure that the interests of working-class civilians were not neglected in all the decisions being taken to create a home front. They were troubled by rising food prices and rents, and were particularly concerned at the welfare of soldier's wives, as it took time for new systems of separation allowances to be designed and implemented. They called for 'a living wage' for soldiers on the war front, which would properly support their dependents at home. In the press and at their meetings, the WWWEC challenged the idea that there was no civilian distress in Walsall. After an active few months at the beginning of the war, the committee died away. Speaking up for the interests of workers on the Walsall home front was left to the local Trades Council until a new organisation was formed in May 1917, the Walsall Labour Vigilance Committee.

Employers and workers, industry and agriculture gradually put themselves onto a war footing in Staffordshire. Each group and each industry had a variety of concerns and a different sense of their own interests. Yet together, they formed the Staffordshire home front.

The War Comes to the Staffordshire Home Front

One way in which people became particularly aware that they were now a home front was when the war directly impinged on their lives in Staffordshire. The interconnection of war and home front became real with the new phenomenon of aerial bombardment of civilians – the Zeppelin raid. Staffordshire was far away from the guns in Flanders or the battles at sea, and yet it too was to be affected by the silver airships. This took many forms: fear of the unknown, the actual experience of bombardment and then the changes in behaviour demanded to protect the population against further raids.

The Staffordshire press contained many references to Zeppelins over the first months of the war, but to begin with there were reports about the fighting in continental Europe. Even when the war came to the home front with the occasional Zeppelin raid on British soil, there was little sense that this was something that the citizens of Staffordshire need worry about. To satisfy their curiosity they could go to the cinema: 'To appreciate fully the gravity of the Zeppelin raid on the East Coast, one should visit the Picture House [Stafford] where the weekend *Pathé Gazette* pictures tell their own story of the death and destruction caused by German aircraft.'[25]

People did not expect to see airships over the county. In May 1915 many around Stafford were startled to see what they thought was a Zeppelin:

Some excitement was occasioned in Stafford and the neighbourhood early on Tuesday morning by the passing of an airship, probably the Army airship *Eta*, over the town … Although the airship was flying a Union Jack and a white ensign, it was evidently regarded by many people as a Zeppelin, and some immediately sought shelter in their cellars. Of course, the airship bore no comparison to a Zeppelin, but it was hardly surprising that those who had never seen an airship before should be supressed with the fear that it was a hostile aircraft.[26]

Some preparations were made just in case. In Wolverhampton, the mayor said that it would be wise to reduce street lighting: 'It would tend to make them safer from Zeppelin raids – though personally he was not nervous about airships coming into the Midlands – and it would be a reminder to the people of the seriousness of the times in which we lived.' However, another speaker pointed out that the lighting of Wolverhampton sank into insignificance beside the tremendous glare from the ironworks at Bilston. Yet people still feared Zeppelin raids. Indeed, when Staffordshire experienced an earthquake on 14 January 1916, people ran out of their houses believing that a Zeppelin had come at last.[27]

Then out of the blue there was a Zeppelin raid on the Midlands (as the papers had to term the target areas). The *Staffordshire Advertiser* commented,

It is obvious that the Midlands must now be included in the danger zone. That Staffordshire would receive a visit from the giant airships probably never entered into the calculations of anyone … Lamentable though the loss of life proved to be, it is surprising that the damage inflicted by a shower of over 300 bombs was not more extensive.

… [T]he public will expect some assurance that every possible precaution will be taken in view of future raids. … [T]he inference may be drawn that those towns which showed the most light received most attention from the enemy. … The raid with its massacre of civilians, including women and children, is on that same plane of that policy of frightfulness that designed the undying infamy which sent the *Lusitania* to its doom and with the introduction of poison gas on the battlefield.[28]

Despite War Office restrictions a considerable amount of detail of how the raid affected Staffordshire appeared in local newspapers, making clear that no military targets had been hit in what appeared to be an unplanned route taken by one of a group of Zeppelins. It was

Damage from Staffordshire's first Zeppelin raid, from *Staffordshire Advertiser*, 12 February 1916.

thought that the culprit had followed – from the air – a train travelling into Staffordshire. Although many bombs fell without causing harm in rural areas, the real damage, injuries and fatalities occurred in urban areas taken unaware. Each town hit had its own terrible story. This was one:

Not very far from the centre of this district is a church separated by a short distance from a meeting-house in which a mission for women and girls was preceeding. A woman missionary ... was standing, Bible in hand, addressing an audience of about 200 persons, mostly women and girls, when a bomb dropped between the church and the mission-room. A hole was left in the ground about 4ft [deep] and 12ft in diameter within 20ft of the mission-room, which was of wood. There was a blinding flash, and then all was darkness.

The woman missionary was struck by a huge fragment of shell and killed instantly. Another lady and a young girl were also killed on the spot. In the darkness the screams of the injured could be heard, and many people were trampled on in the confusion which prevailed for a few moments.

... Some of the victims were killed as they hurried through the streets. In one street a woman and her child lost their lives, while another woman had both legs blown off.

In this Midlands raid, whole families were killed when their homes were struck: a shop assistant was killed as he played billiards in his local saloon; a woman nursing her baby was rescued but the baby died; some escaped with minor injuries when their houses collapsed as they had been drawn into the street to see this unusual sight, but others died because their curiosity took them outside where they were hit by shrapnel. People had no warning and did not know how to respond. Just as it was designed to do, the raid caused panic. People left the picture theatres and other places of amusement while the railway station was closed and train services entirely suspended. Hundreds had to grope their way home in the darkness.[29]

Within days there were a number of responses characteristic of the home front. In one area that was bombed there were said to be six Austrians working at a local shop so 'a movement

ANTI-ZEPPELIN BLINDS. We have Special Facilities for Making and Fixing Blinds of Suitable Dark Materials at a Few Hours' Notice.

JONES, MOSS, & Co., House Furnishers, NEWCASTLE.
COUNTRY HOUSES & PUBLIC BUILDINGS FITTED PROMPTLY, ANY DISTRICT. ESTIMATES GIVEN. TELEPHONE NEWCASTLE 3.

Anti-Zeppelin blinds, from *Staffordshire Advertiser*, 5 February 1916.

has now been set on foot to remove them from the district' and people from miles around came in large numbers to view the damage. Others saw a business opportunity. A house furnisher in Newcastle advertised 'Anti-Zeppelin Blinds', which could be made of suitable dark materials at a few hours' notice. While in one of the towns affected, the coroner's jury returned a verdict of wilful murder against the German emperor.[30]

The fact that there had been a Zeppelin raid on Staffordshire changed daily life on the home front immediately. New routines were required, but what were they to be? A letter in the *Burton Daily Mail* noted that during the recent Zeppelin visit, siren warnings had been given in Derby yet nothing had been done in Burton: 'I know our officials will say the War Office … has declined to notify the approach of hostile aircrafts but are the ratepayers of Burton to be trapped through not having warning? I have yet to meet one person who does not want a warning.' Local authorities discussed how this could be done. The Chief Constable of Stoke-on-Trent said that in future a raid would be signalled by three short blasts from the Corporation works buzzers followed by an interval and then a further three short blasts. After the signal all lights were to be extinguished immediately.[31] Staffordshire people now knew that they had to listen out for danger.

There was a strong suspicion that bright lights created targets for Zeppelins. After the Staffordshire raid, letter writers to the press got busy. Noting how many shops in Stafford were brightly lit on Saturday night, one wrote,

The Home Office Order regarding lighting restrictions is of a stringent character, but it will not operate in this district until Wednesday next. No doubt the German Intelligence Department know this, as well as we do, from their secret agents and spies in Stafford and neighbourhood. What about the intervening nights? Are we to play the German game and continue to show them the way? I hope not.

A direct consequence of the January Zeppelin raid was that lighting restrictions were extended over the whole of Staffordshire and made compulsory. This meant homes, factories, shop windows, railway carriages and trams had to obscure all lights with blinds or curtains so that minimal light was apparent from outside and external lights had to be turned as low as safety permitted. In Staffordshire these restrictions applied from one and a half hours after sunset to an hour before sunrise and were enforced by the police. They reported to the Newcastle Watch Committee that the public were doing their best to comply but 'there was a shortage of dark blinds at the moment'.[32]

However, not everyone was convinced of the necessity for lighting restrictions. When Rugeley UDC discussed the probable implementation of official lighting restrictions in the aftermath of the Midlands raid, one councillor pointed out that more deaths had occurred in London and elsewhere through reduced lighting than by having street lamps lit as usual. The North Staffordshire Traders Association were not happy about the restrictions: one member asked whether one air raid in the Midlands justified the present dismal and dangerous appearance of the streets – 'It had cleared the towns of the purchasing public'. Later that year Burton householders demanded the return of street lighting, arguing against this 'unnecessary darkness'. However, others saw a marketing opportunity. *The Cannock Advertiser* carried an advert:

Darken your windows!
Prudence and Patriotism demand it
Stay at home .... for safety
Get a piano for pleasure
Go to Jones and Co for value
Hednesford.......................................for economy.[33]

It proved hard to maintain the sense of danger. Seven months after the Midlands raid, magistrates felt forced to increase fines in Stoke (to as much as £3) for breaching the Lighting Restriction Order and warned that they intended to be still more severe. It was felt that in the Potteries, 'It is not that there is a deliberate intention to break the law, but simply that offenders do not appreciate the absolute necessity of conformity.' Prosecutions continued throughout the war for showing lights in buildings at night.[34]

The new lighting restrictions also had a range of wider social effects. One was that clocks were no longer illuminated in Newcastle-under-Lyme, which made negotiating public space even more difficult at night. Lighting restrictions also affected everyday shopping. An advert for a Hanley department store from January 1918 pointed out that there was no pleasure in shopping when the streets were in darkness. They therefore proposed to close within the hours of the Restricted Lighting Order, which was 5.30 p.m. at that time of year. People were urged to change their habits and to shop early in the day. Lighting restrictions also affected the timing of shows at local cinemas. Nor did the Armistice bring bright streets once again. Instead, slowly choices were made as to when a neighbourhood could afford to reinstate its street lights. Uttoxeter UDC decided in December 1918 that it could afford to light a further forty-eight lamps now that the war was over.[35]

Back in 1916, the first raid had shaken people. Wilmot Martin, farmer and organiser of a successful wartime concert party, remembered the night of the first Zeppelin:

Photo   MR. MARTIN AND HIS PARTY.   *McCann, Uttoxeter.*
Standing : —Mr. J. Mottram, Miss Hurst, Mr. J. Mitchell, Miss Loveday, M. Leopold Billon, M. van Roeck, Miss L. Leadbetter, Mr. T. Devall.
Sitting —Miss Mottram, Miss E. Bradbury, Mr. W. Martin, Miss R. Harrison, Miss E. Haddon.

The Hixon Concert Party pictured in *Staffordshire Advertiser*, 10 June 1916.

As we neared Stafford we were stopped and ordered to put out our lights, and we found the town entirely in darkness. The people appeared to be greatly alarmed, and were in dread (and so were we) lest the Zeppelins, which were hovering overhead, should drop any bombs. The streets were crowded, and we were expecting all the time to run down somebody. The experience brought most vividly to the minds of the people the awfulness of the war, and helped us to realise more fully the horrors which the troops had to contend with at the Front.[36]

When the next Zeppelins appeared over Staffordshire in late November 1916, there was little damage and few casualties. Warnings had been received and so lights were extinguished and ambulance arrangements made. However, one bomb almost destroyed four houses in Tunstall. Edith Birchall experienced this raid. Her diary entry for 27 November 1916 gives a real sense of what an air raid in First World War Staffordshire was like:

Tonight we retired as usual about 10.30. About 1 o'clock we were awakened by a terrible booming thud which shook the house. For a second I hoped it was a thunderstorm as vivid flashes rent the sky, but it flashed on me that it was a Zeppelin raid and it was fearful to realise that we were in the thick of it. We all jumped out of bed, groped frantically and tremblingly for some clothing and made ourselves go downstairs. There we huddled into a corner farthest away from the window, and listened to the terrible thud of the bombs with our hearts in our mouths as we knew it was as near as possible without breaking the windows. ... We stayed down in the darkness till nearly three o'clock. I then ventured to go to bed. ... About 3.30 the cars started to run again and the street was full of colliers and people.

28 November

After school mother and I went to look at the damage done in Tunstall – a bomb had dropped in a backyard between Sun St and Bond St and made a hole 7 ft deep and a circle 12 ft in diameter. All the property was shattered near and nearly every window was broken in both streets. The zepp. had probably been attracted by the light from Meakins Pottery near to.[37]

This account shows how word spread when the newspapers could not give much specific detail. Edith, as a Zeppelin tourist, found out more by going to look for herself.

Zeppelins seem to have captured the public imagination in Staffordshire, as can be seen in this unusual letter read to the Mid-Staffordshire Appeals Tribunal:

I am sending you this letter to let you know that I wish to withdraw my appeal. My reason for withdrawing it is caused through a dream. My dream was of a Zeppelin raid. In my dream I saw Zeppelins flying overhead. At different intervals I heard explosions, and then I saw buildings on fire. Later on, a gun with several soldiers with it came on the spot, and as I looked at them I saw my brother with them. With constant firing they shot the Zeppelin down. I went to my brother and told him that he was doing wrong in shooting it down, but he did not answer me. He took me by the hand and took me to where the bombs fell, and pointed to a little baby who was brought out from under the ruins of the buildings. It had its arms blown off and badly knocked about. The poor thing was dead. Without speaking to me, he went away and left me there. My dream then ended. On the next morning I had a letter from my brother asking me if I had joined the battery yet. He said that he was not going to trouble to ask me anymore. He has been at the front 11 months. He says that many of them are going to finish next month, as they are on their last month. May I ask you for a favour and get me in his battery. I am quite ready now to go in training, so that I can soon be with him to do my bit to crush such a class of people down. I now know that it is my duty as a Christian to do what I can for poor little children who cannot help themselves.

Here the Zeppelin did not have the intended effect of inducing panic among the civilian population, but persuaded a nineteen year old sewing-machine operator from Stafford, Edgar

Emberton, to change his mind about serving in the Army. Having been called up, Emberton had originally applied for exemption from military service as he objected to 'taking human life as it is contrary to my Religion' which was Church of England. The local Tribunal was not satisfied that he was a bona fide conscientious objector, hence his appeal which he then withdrew after his Zeppelin dream. Subsequently, he was posted with the Stafford Battery, never served abroad and was medically discharged in September 1918.[38]

Emberton was not the only one in Staffordshire to be mesmerised by the 600-foot silver airships. An enterprising railwayman, Mr J. Bayliss, dug up one of the German bombs that had fallen in the Zeppelin raid. He had it photographed to make postcards, which were sold for a penny at local stations and shops. The bomb itself was exhibited and a collection taken. As a result Bayliss raised considerable sums for the Railway Benevolent Institution, funds for local relief and for prisoners in Germany. Meanwhile, in 1917 an exhibition of war relics and curiosities was put on in Uttoxeter, in aid of the fund for eggs for wounded soldiers. Parts of the first Zeppelin to be shot down in England (at Cuffley, Hertfordshire) took pride of place.[39]

The air raids unsettled everyday life, created new anxieties and changed daily behaviour. They also brought home to people in Staffordshire that they were now part of a home front, inextricably connected to the war front. The failings of one would seriously affect the possibility of surviving on the other. One way or another, ordinary life would have to continue now that the county was on a war footing. Moreover, sustaining daily life was only possible if people could find a way to make a living in the unpredictable world of the home front.

CHAPTER THREE

MAKING A LIVING ON THE STAFFORDSHIRE HOME FRONT

Making a living had always been an issue for the people of Staffordshire, but the creation of the home front brought increasing challenges to every household. As men volunteered for the services and local industries moved onto a war footing, the questions for those in Staffordshire were whether their jobs would continue and whether new opportunities would open up, whether wages would be able to keep pace with the increasing cost of living, and how households would manage with the absence of breadwinners.

The challenge for the home front was how to organise local 'manpower' – in fact the labour of men, women, youths and even children – to deliver sufficient recruits for the Army, to provide the labour required for the new war industries that equipped the armed services, to feed both fronts, and to maintain an economy that was resilient enough to finance all these activities. Volunteering might be the quickest way to raise an army but it had an uneven effect on the economic life of the nation with the unplanned removal of key workers, their skills and their wages. Only slowly did government come to recognise that this crisis could not be left to the market but that intervention might be required. All of the new systems to sustain the war and home front were created as the war was being waged. This particularly applied to the management of manpower, which was directed nationally but had to be made to work locally. War affected how individuals and households in Staffordshire made their living and how they did their bit (doing 'your bit' was a popular wartime slogan) for the war.

One issue that was constantly revisited was what trades and which workers were essential to the home front. The Board of Trade's decisions about which occupations should be 'certified', and thus who might be eligible for exemption from military service, changed over the course of the war and could make a difference to an individual and even to a whole town. In April 1916 a mass meeting at Leek Town Hall was called by local trade unions to consider 'the serious position created by the Board of Trade deciding to remove the Silk Trade from the list of certified occupations, which means that practically all single and attested married men of military age, fit for service, can be called up no matter how important their work may be'.[1] They warned that this decision could ruin the trade of the town.

One way in which the public became aware of what constituted work of national importance was the system of badging particular jobs. As more khaki became visible on the home front, the continuing presence of significant numbers of men not in uniform worried some. Stoke Electricity Department decided in May 1915 to issue badges to employees 'to prevent those men being badgered in the town'. The badge indicated that the wearer was employed in public service. Some thought badges were too freely given: at the Central Recruiting Committee for Staffordshire it was said that in Darlaston 'the war badge had been worn there a little too lightly, with the result that a great many men escaped who ought to

LEEK URBAN DISTRICT,

Local Tribunal: Name

Address **TOWN HALL,**

Certificate No. 3898

This is to certify that:— **LEEK.**

Name (*in full*) Joseph Scott.

Address (*in full*) 54 West St Leek

Age 42   Regional No. 406315.

Occupation, profession or business   Bread Baker

is exempted from Military Service.

The exemption is*

up to and including (*date*) November 15. 1918

and on condition that†

The ground (or grounds) on which the exemption is granted is‡

Certified OCCUPATION

Signature   H. Henshaw.

Date 15/4/18   *for the Tribunal.*

* If the exemption is granted on conscientious grounds and is from combatant service only, this should be stated.
† State any conditions, and whether relief from Volunteer Service is granted.
‡ The entry here should be "Occupation," "Education or Training," "Serious hardship," "Ill-health," "Conscientious Objection," or "Certified Occupation," according to the ground (or grounds) on which the exemption has been granted. It is important that all the grounds should be stated.

Joseph Scott's exemption card showing that he was exempted by occupation from military service.

enlist', while another estimated that only 50 per cent of those wearing badges were actually doing war work. By September it was reported to Wolstanton Chamber of Commerce that the Ministry of Munitions was now the sole source of official badges, which were only for skilled men. Their issue was on condition that should the workman leave or undertake employment that was not war work the badge must be returned. There were to be penalties for wearing unofficial badges.[2]

Meanwhile, those in agriculture argued that their employees also ought to be badged as 'security against the reproaches of their neighbours and the recruiting officers'. The Parliamentary Secretary to the Board of Agriculture was forced to explain to the Midland Farmers Association in February 1916:

Badges were reserved absolutely for men who were engaged directly on military work, and once they went beyond this and gave a man a badge because his occupation was important to the country, they would have to give everybody badges and the thing would become meaningless.

However, there remained a view that men would do anything to get the protection of a badge. At the Stafford Tribunal in April 1916 a man employed at a local engineering work claimed that over twenty young men had come into the works during the last three weeks. They had all been given badges while he had been refused one. He said they were agricultural labourers and gardeners who were trying to avoid military service.[3]

With the introduction of conscription in February 1916 came a system to manage the needs of the Army against those of the wartime economy. Men could seek temporary or absolute exemption from military service on grounds of economic hardship to their business or domestic hardship to their family, that they were unfit to serve, had a conscientious objection to war or that they were doing work of national importance. What this meant in local communities was weighed by Local and Appeals Tribunals who could agree or deny exemptions taking advice from a military representative, later a national service representative. The issue of whether badges were needed if one was in a certified occupation also came up at local tribunals. A firm of hardware manufacturers complained to the Walsall Tribunal that they had applied in May for badges for thirty workmen but in July found out that the Badge Department of the Ministry had not authorised them. They pointed out that 70 per cent of the works output was for military purposes. A tribunal member commented, 'What were manufacturers to do if all their workmen were taken from them? The Government could not have both men and munitions.'[4] This, of course, was the nub of the issue for the home front.

Badging was beginning to get a poor reputation and was not a fine enough tool for what the war demanded: the delicate balancing of the needs of the military and the home front. In September 1916, the *Staffordshire Advertiser* had a leader on 'Manpower and Indispensability' where they reported that nationally 1.6 million men of military age had received badges entitling them to exemption. Their view was that tribunals had no power over these men, while there was an even larger number sheltered in government departments and in industry, or 'excused from serving at the front by a whole host of obstructive regulations'. This, they felt, justified the current 'combing out' of young fit men wherever they could be found. The paper asked how many of the vast number of men who were not in khaki were really indispensable to the prosecution of the war. Meanwhile, men whose employers failed to get badges for them could find themselves arrested, fined and handed over to the military authorities, as George Brickwood, a labourer employed by Siemens, discovered to his cost.[5] Soon there was much less talk of badges and badging. Now the focus was on 'combing out'.

Combing out of men who had previously been exempted because of the work they did, their health or their economic circumstances meant that tribunals kept revisiting cases, men were regraded or forced to leave their work of national importance. This could be contentious as was revealed at a case before the Stoke-on-Trent Tribunal in August 1917. Before the war, the man concerned had originally been a miner and had then become a hairdresser, but had continued to work regularly in the pit. In 1915, when his trade as a hairdresser fell off due to the war, he returned to work full time in the colliery. He had then been combed out by the Colliery Recruiting Court. Many in the industry objected to long-serving miners being taken when other less-experienced men were left behind in the pits. However, by this stage of the war, there was a belief in Staffordshire as in other areas with coalfields that becoming a miner was a way of escaping service in the Army. The tribunals had to weigh up the competing value of individual men, their trades and businesses, to the home front or to the Army, while trying to respect local feelings. After well over two years of work, membership of a tribunal was described by one tribunal chairman as 'a very thankless office', although his tribunal was judged to have 'discharged their duties without fear or favour or ill-will'.[6]

One of the challenges for Local and Appeals Tribunals was to balance the needs of industry and agriculture. Farmers in Staffordshire were not always convinced that their importance to the home front was recognised, claiming government regulation was strangling their productivity. By March 1917 the *Tamworth Herald* carried an article that reported a feeling growing among farmers that matters were not in such a dreadful state as the authorities were trying to make out:

anyone who … moves about in the streets of any of our large cities must be struck by the crowds of young men of military age who are going about. They cannot all be medically unfit or in employment of national importance, and in any case they should not be mooching about in the middle of the afternoon, and we want it explained why these are there.

Rather than taking more men from the land, it was suggested men should be combed out from 'non-essential' businesses, leaving alone the reduced staff of the farms. 'We are being worried constantly by every authority from the Premier downward to grow more food, while all the time the men to do the work are being drafted away.' The unfair burden placed on agriculture was echoed in letters complaining about individual cases of men exempted from military service. Sarah Hay of Yoxall wrote in September 1918 complaining about the case of the carrier Herbert Roe, who she thought was 'simply using the carrying business as an excuse for keeping out of the army'. She said, 'The men off the farms have had to go although they were working seven days a week on agriculture while he is left to strut about the roads like a gentleman.'[7]

This belief in unfairness could be found across the home front. In September 1917 a protest at Cannock Urban Tribunal was reported under the headline 'A Monstrous Injustice. Military Service Evaded by Entering Munitions Works'. One tribunal member said that feeling was running high in the district. People were saying, 'my son had had to go into the army, yet others who had been refused exemption are now in munition works'. It was only fair that all men should be treated alike. The tribunal agreed that such men were avoiding their military obligations by obtaining protection certificates. They wanted this to stop. This fitted into a continuing narrative throughout the war that there were among the male workforce slackers who 'stand about on street corners and sometimes sneering at the men who are prepared to go out to fight and save the skins of the very men who snigger at us'. Such judgements were often inflected with class prejudice. In this case, the words come from a businessman active in the Volunteer Training Corps who suggested that he and his colleagues worked twelve to fourteen hours at a stretch. He contrasted this with the working man who, he said, finished his day at four o'clock and then spent 'a third of their time in lounging with their bulging pockets' rather than join the Volunteers.[8]

Individuals and households had to find a way to navigate the increasing regulation of manpower on the home front, if they and their families were to make a living in these unpredictable times.

How Did the War Affect Making a Living on the Staffordshire Home Front?

Making a living in this period was usually a family enterprise with intergenerational dependency: not only were children supported by parents but also many parents could not survive without the wages of their children. By exploring cases from the Mid-Staffordshire Appeals Tribunal we can see how this worked and how the demands of war could threaten the sustainability of households and businesses on the home front.

Households contained a mix of mutual dependencies, which could be disrupted by the removal of one or more of its economically active members, whether sons or husbands or fathers. When Elizabeth Dockerty appealed on behalf of her nineteen-year-old son Henry, who worked as a chauffeur for a local doctor in Uttoxeter, she summarised her case for hardship as '3 other sons gone to the army. My husband owing to illness has not been able to work 18 months. I am solely dependent on this son to keep the home'. Neither Uttoxeter Urban or the Appeals Tribunal were persuaded, yet looking behind the case reveals how the loss to the Army of sons could seriously undermine the viability of a household. In 1911 the Dockerty household consisted of two parents and ten of their twelve living children. Elizabeth did not have a job, but her husband was a bricklayer, and all her sons from Henry upwards at age fourteen brought in a wage as a bricklayer, blacksmith, fitter and store boy, respectively. Her eldest daughter, aged twenty-three, was a lady's maid, but the rest of the five children from age three upwards were economically dependent. By 1916 at least four wages would have been lost with three replaced by the much-smaller Army separation allowances allowed to dependent mothers, provided the sons had been able to make a case on their mother's behalf. The system of separation allowances implemented during the war ensured that economically dependent mothers of soldiers could not receive more than wives (who by definition were understood to be dependent). Their soldier sons had to contribute a proportion of their army pay. In 1916, three more of Elizabeth's children would have reached the age to be economically active but their wages would have been low as they could not yet command the adult rate. Elizabeth's household budget would have consisted of juggling what the children brought in with whatever allowances and pay her enlisted sons could contribute. Having a husband unable to work would have seriously affected the household. Aged fifty-four at the time of the appeal, the effects of manual labour had undermined Thomas's health. He would have had little alternative than to turn to his children if he was to avoid the workhouse.[9]

Adult children often made a significant contribution to the household business and income. The case of Frederick Sleath, market hall keeper and fruiterer in Hednesford, shows how important the contribution of the wider family could be to the viability of a business. His widowed seventy-one-year-old mother was joint owner of the business but she had been an invalid for three years so did not help in the shop. His brother-in-law assisted when not at the colliery and a sister helped in the shop while another did all the buying that Sleath could not do. Two married sisters also gave time to the business without pay, but 'they have a home to look after'. His wife was 'delicate' and could not assist much in the business, although she did run a refreshment stall on Saturdays. The demands of the war meant that the lynchpin of this particular family's economy could be removed to serve in the Army. Others prepared for what they saw as the inevitable. In response to his call-up, a forty-year-old milk seller trained two

Fryer's fruit shop in Stafford.

A typical village store in Brewood that was both a grocers and boot dealer, *c.* 1900.

of his four daughters to deliver the milk on his round in Stafford so that it could continue in his absence. His only son was in the Army and his wife was an invalid.[10]

Some tribunal cases show how a household aggregated a number of wages or parts of wages to produce a single household income. The Spinks family of Hednesford appear in the Appeals papers through the case of Fred, aged nineteen, a boot salesman at a store in Walsall. He lived at home with his widowed mother and his grandfather plus sister and a collier brother, who was about to get married. Three of his brothers were serving at the front having volunteered early in the war. In addition his sister was married to a soldier who had been wounded. Mrs Spinks felt 'she was entitled to favourable consideration' as four members of her family were serving. However, Lord Hatherton, military representative at the tribunal, then commented, 'and two at home'. The tribunal was as interested in the financial consequences for the Spinks family of the changes the war had brought. Fred partially maintained the household by 'turning up' all his wage of 22*s*, while his older and about-to-be-married collier brother gave up some of his (7*s* 6*d*). His grandfather was too old at seventy-two to contribute and his mother looked after home. His married sister lived with them and received a full separation allowance for herself and her children of 17*s* 6*d*. A further 1*s* 9*d* was added for the mother by one of the sons at the front. The local tribunal felt a case of hardship was demonstrated and therefore chose not at this stage to enquire into Fred's conscientious objection to military service. He was granted one month's temporary exemption. However, the military representative who appealed against this decision felt there was no sufficient evidence of serious hardship in view of the separation allowance and the fact that a brother and sister were living at home. His appeal was lost but there seems to have been no further case seeking exemption for Fred. The family would have had to manage on a severely depleted income. Sadly, Private Fred Spinks of the Lincolnshire Regiment, who had enlisted at Hednesford, was killed in action on the

Western Front on 23 March 1918. It is not clear whether his conscientious objection to war was ever acknowledged.[11]

Many married men on the Staffordshire home front supported their widowed mothers alongside a dependent wife and children. A thirty-six-year-old pawnbroker's manager ran the business in Hednesford for his widowed mother. She was fifty-nine and 'suffers badly' from varicose veins and bronchitis and could not 'think of taking the whole responsibility of the business'. There were also many delicate wives. This was important because the case was being made that they could not step into their husband's shoes to continue business or to provide equivalent economic support. The wife of a grocer in Wimblebury was not strong and, importantly, there were no relations who could help her. It was the family to whom you were expected to turn in hard times. Support of dependent parents was apparent across the social scale. A master draper who had four shops, mostly in Burton-on-Trent, argued in November 1917, 'To close my four shops now would mean great hardship for my Father, Mother and wife and ruination for myself, and a great loss to the town in rates, taxes and employment.'[12]

Economic dependency could also extend beyond kin relationships. Employers could even feel obligations beyond the lifetime of their employees. The case made for Herbert Smith, a waggoner from Ellenhall, revealed the extent of his employer's commitments. The farmer had had a waggoner who enlisted – he was married with ten children. When the man came back on leave he had hung himself, so now the farmer was maintaining this man's family too. Others created economic bonds as a way to try to survive the challenges of the war. Many men worried about what would become of their business if they went into the Army. Some made arrangements with colleagues and even rival businesses to ensure that there would be something to support their family while they were away and a livelihood to return to at the war's end. James Howells, a Tamworth bootmaker, revealed in 1917 to the local tribunal that '2 years ago I encouraged G. Grey to join the Army and E. Sommers 18 months ago, by

Sproston's gentlemen's outfitters shop in Stafford, *c*. 1910.

promising should they return their places would be open'. Howells argued that if he now had to join up then three men would have no livelihood to return to as his business would have gone.[13]

Given these webs of dependency it is not surprising that men living on the Staffordshire home front faced pressure to only undertake work that directly contributed to the war effort. Before conscription was introduced, there was moral pressure to take up work of national importance. Speaking to Tamworth RDC, the mayor said that council employees who were wanted for making munitions should be made to go, and if they refused then they should be sacked. The local Labour Council protested, 'because the men happened to be servants of the public they ought not to be badgered or driven in a different manner to the people who were employed by the private employer'. Men changed their occupations either because of instructions from the tribunals or in anticipation of their call-up. A grocer's assistant who worked for Tamworth Co-op and who had been rejected three times by the Army, was directed to do work of national importance. From December 1917, he was employed as a waggoner on an 80-acre farm. Some transfers were in the opposite direction. Joseph Thompson had been employed in farm work and had then become a tram motorman, but sought to move back into agriculture when he was called up in September 1918. He had a wife and six children. Because of the serious shortage of skilled ploughman, it was made clear to him that if he could convince the War Agriculture Executive Committee (WAEC) and the Sedgley Tribunal then he might receive an exemption and therefore permission to transfer back to farm work. A local farmer was willing to give him work as Thompson already had nine years' experience in farm work and could not only plough but also work as a cowman or waggoner. However, this was not the end of the story. The WAEC decided his age and health (thirty-four, Grade 1) overrode his possible contribution to food production and therefore could not support his exemption. Meanwhile, Thompson said that he had decided to leave farm work as he found it impossible to keep his large family on meagre agricultural wages.[14]

The war meant that many men juggled more than one job as they tried to make a living or endeavoured to make their employment fit new definitions of work in the national interest. Some carried into the war a demanding combination of jobs. Frederick Bloor of Leek had in 1918 been working full time for twenty-three years as a silk dyer's labourer while at the same time running his own business as a wholesale and retail newsagent. He worked as a newsagent from 7 to 8.30 a.m. and from 6.15 to 9 p.m. on weekdays and then Saturday afternoons until 10 p.m., and all Sundays. His son had assisted him in the business but he had been lost on HMS *Hampshire*. Although Bloor's two eldest daughters were married, he was still supporting six children under seventeen. Others combined jobs such as a wholesale fruit and potato merchant who was also a scrap metal dealer; a baker who was also a postman as well as keeping six pigs and a large garden; or a man who combined being a hairdresser and a tobacconist. Running a smallholding besides a job was not uncommon, such as a provision hand at the Tamworth Co-op who also tended nearly 2 acres with pigs and poultry. The demands of the war encouraged such sidelines. The war was also apparent in a number of cases where men combined working in a colliery with running their own businesses. William Millington ran a grocery shop in Chadsmoor, which he had recently begun to combine with working six days a week down the pit. He then worked evenings and Saturday afternoon at his shop in order to support his wife, child and widowed mother. He had previously been an insurance agent as well as a grocer. The military representative saw this as a deliberate attempt to thwart his call-up: 'if this kind of thing is allowed it will be impossible to satisfactorily work the Act in this district and that is most subversive to the National Interest'.[15]

Even when not doing multiple jobs, many on the home front worked long hours. John Parker explained to the Cannock Tribunal that he was now working from 6 a.m. to 9 p.m.

daily as a plumber and decorator as he was the only skilled man left in his business, which normally employed six men. All he had by July 1916 was two boys to assist him. In November 1917, the Lichfield City Tribunal heard a case of a man who was working seventy-two hours a week. The national service representative told the man's employer, 'Have you seen in the papers that a movement is on foot to get men to work less hours and do more work? ... Your customers would be better served if the man worked less hours'.[16]

The other way for a family to make ends meet and for local businesses to continue with significant labour shortages on the home front was to draw new workers into the labour market.

New Work and New Workers on the Home Front

The home front created new kinds of work not needed on such a scale or even at all in peacetime, such as munitions. In addition the labour shortages generated by large numbers of workers volunteering and later being conscripted into the armed services created opportunities. However, in many corners of Staffordshire there was reluctance to employ untested women, with preference being given particularly in agriculture to boys or to prisoners of war (POWs). Indeed, by January 1918 a new presence was noted in the fields of Staffordshire: the men in field grey (the colour of the German uniform). These were some of the forty gangs of German POWs now working in Mid Staffordshire.[17]

Women in Staffordshire recognised what was required of them on a home front but, as elsewhere in the country, often found they had to argue for their 'right to serve'. Nine months into the war, a Walsall woman argued: 'Women are the home keepers, but they are burning to help England, and, given the opportunity, will rise to the emergency and do double duty in the hour, now, when it is needed'.

However, there was resistance from many quarters. A woman described as strong and quite equal to the work wanted to be a tram conductor in Walsall, but in May 1915 it seemed that rather than employ women, young men were being used to fill the vacancies created by enlisted men. The suggestion was made:

If these men enlisted, and the authorities promised to keep their berths open for them, many young women in Walsall would, I am sure, come forward to take their places, women not now industrially employed, or only so for short hours. ... Women could be put to work after a week's initiation or less, providing that a sensible clerk could be given latitude as to arranging hours ... The elderly men retained could run the early morning and late night cars.[18]

Trade unions, from which women had largely been excluded except for the new general unions, had to decide what to do in these new circumstances. When the Midland Counties Trades Federation met in May 1915, it was reported that there were 30,000 trade unionists in Walsall. A great effort had been made to organise female labour and now 1,000 women were unionised, the majority of whom were receiving equal wages with men for equal work.[19] This was increasingly seen as the only way to protect male wage rates in the longer term, given that traditionally women's pay was only a fraction of the male rate. The fear was that if employers got used to hiring lower-paid women during the war, the returning soldiers would not get their jobs back come the peace.

There was increasing pressure on women to volunteer for new kinds of war work such as munitions. In April 1916 a trade unionist lamented the effect on Leek's silk industry of 'two thousand married women ... who were to leave their homes and kiddies and be shipped to Manchester or Birmingham on munition work. It was ridiculous'. In February 1917 the *Leek Times* carried a notice:

A studio portrait of women munition workers employed at Siemen's Engineering Works, Stafford.

Girls wanted urgently for shell-filling at the Coventry and Hereford factories. Good inducements are offered as far as wages are concerned, the rate being from 25s to 35s per week. Those willing to help the country in this way should volunteer at once by applying to the Manager, Labour Exchange, Derby St.

This request was reinforced from local pulpits where, at the request of the Board of Trade, an appeal was made for girls to volunteer for shell filling. Nor was it just in Leek. The *Tamworth Herald* carried a large advert in May 1917 calling for 500 women to work as machine operators in a large shell-making factory, working day or night shifts. No one resident more than 10 miles from Birmingham was eligible nor anyone at present engaged in government work, as you could not change jobs in controlled establishments engaged in war work without official sanction. Good living accommodation was highlighted in lodgings and in the hostel attached to the works. The advert had been placed by the Austin Motor Co., Longbridge, Birmingham.[20]

Although it took time, by 1917 some parts of the county were congratulating themselves on the numbers of women who were now doing men's jobs. In the Potteries, it was claimed that they were one of the first districts in the country to employ women as taxicab drivers. It was not uncommon to see tradesmen's motor delivery vans and private cars driven by women. Women billposters and window cleaners on the top of high ladders could also be seen. On the electric tramways women had been acting as conductors for many months and very few, even of old and ineligible men, were now employed in this work. 'The pluck they have shown in facing the discomforts of the severest winter experienced for many years has been splendid'.[21]

All sides of industry and agriculture debated the suitability of women for particular kinds of work, particularly for skilled or hard manual labour. At the Stoke Tribunal in April 1917,

New work for women: a telegram delivery woman in Stafford.

when considering a large firm of wholesale grocers, the military representative emphasised that the Army's urgent need for men meant that businesses must dilute their labour further (that is break up skilled jobs into a series of less-skilled tasks) and employ more women. When the employer said that it was quite impossible for women to drag about big sides of bacon, the representative said he knew of women doing work just as heavy in hauling timber. If the applicant wished to continue his business, he would have to employ women. In commenting on this case, a columnist in the *Staffordshire Advertiser* said that he had recently seen women assisting in repairing the tramway track in one of the Potteries' towns. His view was that 'In normal times it would be impossible, on many grounds, to defend the employment of women in what may be termed the heavy grades of labour, but in war time, when manpower is so urgently needed for the Army and for national service, such measures must be justified.'[22]

Yet, many could not see how their business or farm could possibly adapt to these new strictures, whatever the moral and official pressure. Agriculture was widely believed to be particularly conservative in this respect. At the Staffordshire War Agriculture Committee, the issue was much discussed. In June 1917 one WAC member noted:

In Staffordshire there was a strong and traditional prejudice against women labour. There were plenty of women available to help during the harvest who had not been asked to assist and who would do so if they were approached. He believed that if they could break down the prejudice that existed in Staffordshire against the employment of women labour half the problem of labour shortage on the land would be solved.

Hard manual work undertaken by women: women railway workers at Stafford.

A group of Staffordshire women training to do farm work, *Staffordshire Advertiser*, 6 October 1917.

However, another member said that in his experience women could do some work well on the farm, but they could not do it all. At tribunals many military representatives appeared to be very encouraging of women's labour, although for most this was more as a convenient means to release men for the Army than from any recognition of women's equal capacities. At one case when a farmer finally admitted he could not employ women because he preferred a man, the military representative said, 'I agree with you, but we are now at a time when we must make the best of things, and if you can't get men you must employ women.'[23]

Resistance to women taking on new jobs often focused on their lack of experience compared to the men they were replacing. Providing training for potential substitute workers became increasingly important as the war continued. Staffordshire Education Committee developed a scheme in cooperation with farmers to offer instruction to women in milking and other light branches of farm work. The county began to encourage women's employment on the land in 1915 but it was not until March 1917 that this gained a real impetus with the formation of the Women's War Agriculture Committee (WWAC). The WWAC had local committees, such as at Uttoxeter, as well as village committees set up in conjunction with another wartime innovation, the Women's Institute, as in Marchington. By October 1917 WWAC was reporting slow but real progress, although it mainly consisted of a lone woman working on a hay-baler or girls being used for potato digging. The pace of recruitment picked up in the first half of 1918, with 919 recruits called up of whom 432 were accepted. In this group, 81 were placed on farms, 124 into training, 93 sent to other counties and 118

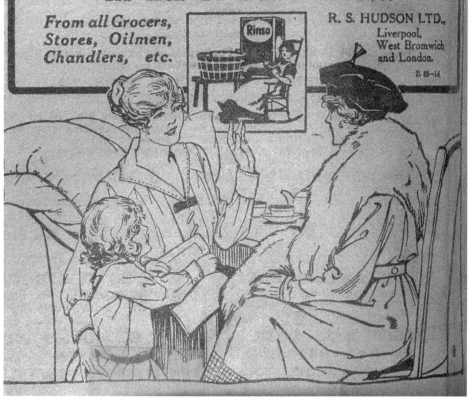

Adverts show the changes that war brought to the home front. Rinso, the dirt dispeller, helps you do the washing yourself when the maid has left to become a munitions worker, *Staffordshire Advertiser*, 7 July 1917.

transferred to the timber supply or forage department. Individual women were sent for six weeks training at the Midland Agricultural and Dairy College. Regular reports now appeared in the press describing the activities of small gangs of women potato picking or harvesting fruit or hay-baling. Despite the evident conservatism of many Staffordshire farmers, in time the new land girls proved their value. By August 1918 a member of Cannock Rural Tribunal admitted, 'The condition of the land was a testament to the girls' work, being full of fine produce'.[24]

The issue remained whether the demands of the war could unsettle traditional assumptions about what was appropriate work for women. There were many examples where it suited tribunals to press reluctant husbands to turn to their wives to take over their business. These were women often described as delicate or otherwise unable to work. John Whitehead, who ran a grocery in Tamworth, said his wife was seriously ill and could not manage the business. He said, 'I have also endeavoured to train a lady assistant but I have found it impossible to succeed in this direction.' Others suggested that they would have to compromise on their business practices if they employed women. The Great Western and Metropolitan Dairies, who had a condensing factory at Weston, argued that the Home Office would not allow them to work women in the way they employed men. They complained that women could only work for sixty hours a week and they had to have one day's rest. They clearly felt this was unreasonable. They could not envisage a woman replacing their skilled head cheesemaker, who also supervised the night shift.[25]

With clerical work, the concern was not the strength of women but their skill, despite evidence that they were the backbone of much of the wartime bureaucracy. At an appeal brought on behalf of a clerk who prepared income tax returns, Eustace Joy suggested the firm should get some lady clerks but they could only imagine using them for copying work or dictating letters. Joy replied that he employed at least twenty lady clerks, some for routine duties but others 'were doing really good, serious work'. At Tamworth, a tribunal case concerning the assistant clerk to the Board of Guardians focused on whether it was possible to replace him with a woman. One member suggested 'that a girl would "jump into the work in no time"' but the clerk to the Guardians said he was surprised at such a remark: 'A woman could not do it without years of training. It requires a great deal of technical knowledge.' The mayor responded that 'it was surprising what ladies could do'. Wartime also prompted commercial training for young women to meet the needs of the home front but also in anticipation of opportunities when peace came. Arthur Bailey claimed that in the first three months of 1916 his shorthand – typewriting school in Burton had obtained posts in business offices for forty-nine lady students. His tribunal case revealed that the wide demand for trained clerical staff on the home front was being met by classes for women offered by Staffordshire Education Committee as well as private providers like the school that Bailey ran in rooms at Burton's YMCA.[26]

Some found it hard to imagine women taking on particular tasks. The idea of waged, trained and uniformed police women was a step too far for many. When it was proposed to appoint two police women in Walsall, some councillors were beside themselves. One argued, 'If there were any women to spare, their places should be in the factories, and he was not in favour of them "having fancy jobs and walking about the streets in uniform".' In the same vein the manager of a chain of meat shops said at Stafford Borough Tribunal that he was not prepared to employ female labour as he did not think it was women's place to handle meat, to which a member of the tribunal replied, 'The women have to cook it.' However, others were quite open to women doing work usually seen as male. Cannock Rural Tribunal heard from a Cheslyn Hay blacksmith that he had a woman working for him as a striker and she was better at the work than many men.[27]

Early in the war some warned that how new women workers were treated would matter for the conduct of the war. Pay was to be a crucial issue. Women had traditionally been

Burton Daily Mail

AY, MARCH 3, 1916.

BAILEY'S
SHORTHAND-TYPEWRITING SCHOOL.
ROOMS 1, 2, 3, Y.M.C.A.

PRINCIPAL:—Mr. Arthur Bailey, F.Inc.S.T., F.C.T.S., M.N.S.A., P.C.T.

OTHER SUBJECTS.—Book-keeping, Commercial Correspondence, Business Methods, French.

CONVENIENT CLASSES.—Day and Evening. Hours: 9—12; 2—9. Beginners started at once—any day, any time. Students of Typewriting learn on latest model Underwoods—the machines most popular with the employers of Britain and Burton. The Touch System only is taught by the most successful modern method. Shorthand and Typewriting or Book-keeping and Typewriting are learned by intelligent and energetic workers in three months.

TERMS.—Lower non-State-aided terms do not exist. Efficiency having been secured, all profits will go to the Relief Funds.

APPOINTMENTS.—Forty-nine students obtained posts during the last three months. Good and permanent appointments are absolutely assured to experts. War economy will demand, and employers will prefer them.

FUTURE DEMANDS.—Militarism begets militarism. Never again will Great Britain trust the peaceful intentions of envious Continental rivals armed to the teeth. THEREFORE her great National Army has come to STAY, as the late Lord Roberts, with characteristic foresight, said it would. Hence also there will be an unprecedented and continuous demand for Lady, Boy, and Girl Clerks AFTER the war; but happy the parents whose boys and girls are earning something in the long lean years immediately ahead.

An advert for Arthur Bailey's shorthand and typing school, Appeals Case 257.

poorly paid as they were not assumed to be supporting dependents. The war changed this and increased demands for equal pay. Yet there was a common perception that women got particularly good wages if they worked in a munitions factory. At the Walsall Tribunal, a partner in a boot and shoe retailer said 'women are getting so much money in munition factories that it is impossible to get them into shops'. The military representative suggested that the firm should give the women as good wages. The astonished reply was, 'You cannot pay them 35s per week.' Women's low pay was a key feature of the Staffordhsire home front, as elsewhere. Miss Lawley, women's trade union organiser, observed that women workers in Uttoxeter were being paid considerably below the scale. Others argued that the higher wages available to women munition workers (which were still significantly lower than male rates) should be used to drive up women's low pay. The Stafford branch of the National Federation of Women Workers passed a resolution:

In view of the statement in the Press that agriculture is of as great national importance as the manufacture of munitions, this meeting composed of women munition workers, protests against the low rate of wages paid to the women on the land.

It is therefore not surprising that, in order to contribute to the household income or to support themselves, many young women would travel some distance from their homes in Staffordshire to get munitions work. A murder case in March 1918 revealed that Minnie Astbury, the twenty-four-year-old victim from Hanley, had been a munition worker for two years at Kynoch's in Birmingham. Her fellow lodgers were also women munition workers from the Potteries.[28]

The paucity of local wage rates for young women, in particular, was evident in Appeals cases where mothers claimed they could not survive on their daughter's wages if their better-paid sons were forced into the Army. Separation allowances were not regarded as sufficient to compensate for the loss of an adult male's wage. Among the cases of people summoned in Stafford for non-payment of the poor-rate in September 1915 was a woman who explained how difficult it was to manage on a separation allowance. Before the war her husband earned anything from £1 to 36s a week, but since his enlistment she had only 12s 6d separation allowance. From that she had to pay 3s rent, 2s 6d for furniture, 2s 6d for coal and 1s 7d for insurance. She struggled to make ends meet as she was unable to work through ill health. Many women found themselves in similar circumstances. Court cases began to appear of fraudulent claims for separation allowances. In Rugeley, a khaki-clad mining engineer was charged with bigamy in July 1918. He had fraudulently appropriated nearly £72 in separation allowances on behalf of a second wife while his real wife was getting an allowance. The judge said that there were three women with whom this man had gone through the ceremony of marriage. He was sentenced to one year's imprisonment. However, for others the separation allowance was an improvement on their dire circumstances. One Appeals case concerned a young single man who cared for his invalid mother. Their sole income was the mother's old age pension of 5s and around 2s 6d profit on a small business she had. The son's appeal was dismissed with a tribunal member telling him that his mother would be much better off with the Army allowance.[29]

Although women workers were a key part of the Staffordshire home front, another group were also asked to make a contribution – children. In many cases employers viewed boy labour more favourably than women. What was contentious was whether the war justified the early curtailment of boys' education so that they could enter the labour market. At the end of 1914, the Staffordshire Education Committee was asked to make a special case to release thirteen- and fourteen-year-old boys from school in Darlaston to assist manufacturers

Potential workers: a school photograph from Weaton Aston.

in executing orders for the Army and Navy, as so many local men had enlisted. The employers said that 60 per cent of the work done at Darlaston was for the military; however, 20 per cent of their male workforce had already enlisted. At this stage the Education Committee, who had to sanction this, took the view that other places in the county were engaged in war contracts but Darlaston was the only one applying to use boy labour. Some on the committee said that if the Darlaston manufacturers would pay the price for adult labour, then they would not need to turn to boys.[30]

Yet by the end of 1915, the Education Committee had released hundreds of boys and girls over twelve years of age from school attendance in the rural districts so that they could engage in farm work. As the war went on, farmers were able to apply to release named boys from school so that they could be employed in agriculture. This did not always work well as was shown by a case before Penkridge Police Court in October 1918. The labour of Walter Houghton, now fourteen, had been secured when he was twelve by John Burton, a farmer. He was paid 5s a week with pocket money and lived in. However, Houghton left the farm without giving notice and the farmer sued him for damages caused by absenting himself from work. The farmer had had to engage two women, one at 25s and the other at 10s a week, in order to get the milking done. The boy's father said that Walter had served twelve months and he did not consider that any notice was necessary. He added that the boy had been working very long hours. The magistrate, Lord Hatherton, did not choose to comment on what seemed to be the exploitation of child labour, instead taking the view that 'the lad took advantage of his employer's good nature, who had obtained exemption for him, to leave his service and go into munition works, where he could earn more money'. The boy was ordered to pay £3 with 12s costs.[31]

Agriculture was not the only industry that found boy labour useful. Mining had traditionally seen youths employed, but the greatest mining disaster of wartime Staffordshire at Minnie Pit, Halmerend, on 12 January 1918 revealed quite how extensive the employment of boys was. It was noted,

A remarkable feature of the disaster is that the great majority of the victims are young men and boys, and that at least half a dozen of the latter had only commenced to work in the pit on the previous Monday. There is hardly a house in Halmerend and the surrounding villages which is not in mourning, and in some cases fathers and sons have gone.

Among the 155 dead were boys of fourteen.[32]

Individuals and households had to negotiate the changing demands for managing manpower on the home front if they were to continue to make a living and support those who were economically dependent. Businesses also had to adapt if they were to survive on the home front.

The Effect of the War on One Business: Maskery's (bakers), Leek

Maskery's was a family bakery established in Leek in 1796. In 1911, it was run by seventy-five-year-old Thomas Maskery. He lived with his wife Jane (aged sixty-eight) of no stated occupation. Four of their adult children lived at home together with the Maskerys' grandson, Frank Reginald, who was twenty-one and a confectioner. The four children consisted of their eldest son Frank, forty-eight, an accountant; Harry, aged forty-two, confectioner; Hannah, forty-one, assistant in a shop; and Lizzie, thirty-nine, no occupation. Thomas Maskery died in 1913 and his widow took over the business. It was in her name that all the applications were made on behalf of Maskery's workers for exemption from military service. However, she does not seem to be an example of a woman whom the demands of war forced into business, as she was not the day-to-day manager of Maskery's.[33]

At the outbreak of war Maskery's was a bakery and provisions dealer that, in addition to family members, employed six bakers and one van man as well as assistants in its shop

A postcard showing Maskery's bakers and their van man, used in the appeal for exemption made for George Astles.

and tearoom. In mid-1916 the bakery supplied twelve shops in Leek and a further six in the country. They had had to turn down other requests to supply similar shops.

The attrition of experienced bakers happened gradually. By the end of 1915 three bakers had volunteered or 'gone' as was written across each of the men on a postcard showing Maskery's workforce that was found in their solicitor's papers. The card shows the situation at the time of the application by George Astles, the van man, and was used to give a visual representation of how the war had affected the bakery. Maskery's was already having problems replacing the men who had enlisted. In August 1916 the bakers were Jane's grandson Frank R. Maskery (aged twenty-six, who had been rejected for military service), Joseph Scott (aged thirty-nine, also rejected due to being ill at times for two to three weeks with foot trouble), and James Coe (aged twenty-five, category A). A case was made by Maskery's to the local tribunal on behalf of Coe. He was the sole support of a widowed mother and also kept his sister as she only got 15s a week for her munitions work. After an initial three-month exemption, the attempt to extend this failed and he was called up, serving in France from June to September 1917 as an infantryman and baker. Most of the rest of his war was spent in various hospitals in England and Ireland with trench fever and then two bouts of gonorrhoea.

His loss deeply affected the business, as Jane Maskery commented, 'it is beyond endurance for men to do more work than these men are doing'. By summer 1916, Maskery's was advertising for staff just like other Staffordshire bakeries. Others sought youths and even adult men, but Maskery's was looking for ladies: 'WANTED Lady for Bakehouse; experienced in all kinds of Fancies. Also experienced Lady for Counter; good wages. T. Maskery, Confectioner Leek'.[34] This advert was still appearing at the end of 1917, which suggests that as Jane Maskery said of her missing male bakers, 'it is impossible to replace them'. In the case she made to keep Scott, it was stated that, 'The ladies only make fancy cakes', they did not make bread. Moreover, at this point it was noted of the women employed that they could not make sponge cakes or work the machine for pies – that is, it was being argued, women could not substitute for bakers. As a result the remaining bakers had to work long hours – Frank worked seventy hours a week in the bakehouse. Of course, those who were not eligible for call-up were also in the workforce. Harry Maskery (one of Jane's sons, forty-nine in 1918) was a baker of cakes but he was actually at home, 'bad' with heart trouble and in April 1918 it was noted that he only did about one hour a day and was going away for his health.

Harry Maskery's work also shows that the business even in wartime was more than the making and distribution of bread. However, that remained at the centre of the business. In 1918 they calculated that with two remaining bakers, Frank R. Maskery and Scott (now graded at C3), and with one van man also now graded at C3, the business produced 4,000 loaves a week. Frank essentially ran the business as foreman baker as Jane Maskery said that at seventy-four years old 'she cannot now take an active part'. By 1916 Frank was responsible for the business, specifically the weighing, measuring, mixing and proper baking. This was to become increasingly demanding as official restrictions grew on how bread was to be prepared, with what ingredients, at specific weights and in particular conditions. Any deviation from these standards resulted in prosecutions – the local newspapers were full of them – which could in turn jeopardise the business and the livelihoods of all the employees, particularly those for whom their occupation was what was allowing them to be exempted from military service.

In the case of Maskery's van man, we get a glimpse of an ordinary family's experience of the home front. George Astles was a van man and assistant, who had been employed by Maskery's since he was seventeen. In 1918 he was twenty-eight and married with one child. He had originally been rejected by the Army and was given a certificate of discharge in 1916. But then he was categorised as B2 in 1917, then C3, then Grade 3. Imagine the pressure

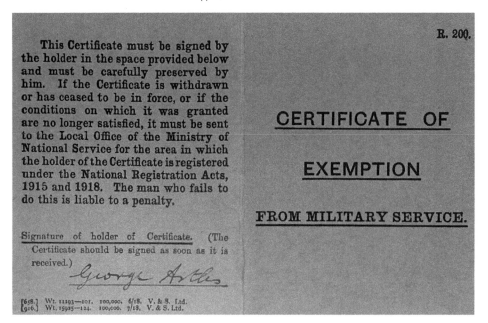

George Astles' exemption card.

that put on him and his family as well as the business as the goalposts kept shifting. He had asthma and was considered to be unfit for military service, but Jane Maskery's case on his behalf focused on the grounds of occupation. His case appeared on four occasions before the Leek Tribunal gaining further exemptions of a few months each time. There was another wage coming into his household. In 1910, he had married Lily who worked as a silk winder even when their son was two months old. In the tribunal cases he was not described as a baker, although in the 1911 census he was, and after the war he was described as a baker and later as a confectioner (cakes). Astles must have continued to be important to Maskery's as he was a pall bearer at Frank Maskery senior's funeral in 1933. After the war an event occurred that seems to show the effects of living with the uncertainty of whether George would be forced into the Army. In December 1921 the body of his wife was recovered from the canal. The verdict was suicide; it was noted that she had suffered from depression of late. She was thirty years old.

Maskery's managed to adapt and survive the challenges of the war, contributing men to the armed services while maintaining sufficient workers (just) to maintain the business. However, what it meant to be a bakery and confectionery business changed. When all decisions seemed provisional, the strain of this must have been considerable. This was not necessarily the same as worrying about the lives of men at the front, but it was still stressful. The pervasiveness of these kind of daily anxieties explains the continuing attraction of anything that could take your mind off your worries, whether it was concert parties, the cinema, spiritualist sessions or a cup of tea and even a cake at Maskery's tearooms. All were part of the Staffordshire home front.

Maskery's seem to have been relatively unusual among Staffordshire businesses in its openness to hire women. However, in many ways the war did not challenge the sexual division of labour or definitions of skill. The local press and Appeals cases show that when it came to bakeries, there was a clear demarcation of jobs. Dough cutting was a different skill to moulding and was claimed to be harder work. There was also a

Bebbington's bread delivery van, Stafford, 1917.

difference between the van man and those who actually made the bread. Bread delivery men (there is no evidence of women doing this job) were also advertised for: 'BAKERS – Bread salesman – able to drive Ford; make new trade on existing Country journeys; permanency to steady man; Wolverhampton district'. Moreover, bakers did not just make bread:

Mr Hill's shop at Queensville is a frequent place of call for our soldiers in training. Cakes and confectionery always await the visitor ... Rowlands bread is supplied. Biscuits and other edibles are stocked, so that those who pass by may find something here to suit their taste.[35]

However, as we have seen, the creation of 'fancies' was often considered to be women's work.

What Maskery's experience shows is that what it meant to be a baker changed as the war wore on. The local press had more and more bread-related stories and reports. As the challenges of food shortages bit, and the decision was taken by government not to ration bread but to deal with shortages of wheat by having an anti-waste campaign, adulterating wheat with other grains, and curbing consumption by campaigns to eat less bread and to only sell it when it was stale, bakers became more valuable to the home front. Military representatives challenged the continuing exemptions of men like Frank Maskery but they did not always persuade tribunals. Applicants increasingly underlined, as was reported at one tribunal case in Tamworth, that 'the military were "hoggish", they wanted every man ... [But] People had to be supplied with bread'.[36] Jane Maskery's case to keep Astles was justified with 'regard to the importance of the food supply'. The responsibility for finding a way to create palatable and saleable bread of the right weight and with approved ingredients was the bakers, and this put them under considerable pressure.

Unlike Maskery's, many bakery businesses did not survive the war. In 1917 it was reported that eight bakers in Tamworth had been compelled to give up or had gone to the wall. Baking bread was now undertaken by fewer staff, often less skilled, to far more exacting regulations but where additional costs could not be passed on to the customer. The effect of this on the home front's remaining bakers was underlined by the local secretary of the bakers' trade union, the Operative Bakers and Confectioners' Society. In August 1918 Herbert Emery said,

the position among the bakers had become critical, the trade having been practically drained, one-third of the men in the trade having been taken for the Army. … many men were working 20 hours a week overtime, with the result that there was an abnormal percentage of sickness. The men felt that the trade had done its duty.[37]

These kind of grievances about work conditions festered on into the peace so that in 1919 there was a bakers' strike that reportedly led to a bread famine in the Potteries and long bread queues, reminiscent of the war, in Stafford.

The story of Maskery's shows how one firm responded to the challenge of making a living in the unpredictable environment of the home front. In the absence of many breadwinners, it was employers, workers, and those who had traditionally not engaged in paid labour that had to adapt to the new demands of the home front. In turn, maintaining households so that as many of their members as possible could contribute to the war economy was what would ensure the resilience of the home front. The Staffordshire home front rose to these challenges with differing effects on particular individuals, households and businesses. However, this was not the end of exhortations to civilians to do 'your bit' in this new kind of warfare.

CHAPTER FOUR

'DOING THEIR BIT': VOLUNTEERING ON THE HOME FRONT

Volunteering on the home front varied from knitting socks for soldiers or buying flags to support the Red Cross through to providing unpaid labour for the war effort as a nursing auxiliary or serving on one of the many wartime committees that organised the home front. All these activities had the capacity to display patriotic support for soldiers at the front, to show sacrifices could be made at home and to plug gaps in the manpower crisis.

One of the earliest calls for voluntary action came with the refugee crisis created by the German invasion of Belgium. Across the county appeals were made for accommodation and funds to provide hospitality for refugees. Generosity was apparent everywhere. In Tutbury the Misses Richardson of the Girls' School took a five-roomed cottage in the High Street and their pupils undertook to pay the rent for a Belgian family. Everyone in the village tried to provide something. Farmers gave sacks of potatoes and apples while a grocer donated provisions. The more well-to-do were able to house refugees, like the Hon Walter and Mrs Yarde-Buller, who welcomed Belgian refugees to their home in the village of Marchington. It was noted that everything needed for the comfort of strangers was being contributed by the public. Local businesses also did their bit. In Burton, the Bass brewery rented and furnished two houses in Craven Street where they maintained refugee families.[1]

Refugees arrived with no resources and their upkeep was provided by regular voluntary subscriptions. These were managed by local Belgian Refugee Relief committees. Towards the end of the war key figures within Staffordshire's network of support were officially recognised. The King of the Belgians conferred the Medal of Queen Elizabeth on Miss Ethel Parker-Jervis for the valuable services she rendered to Belgian refugees and soldiers during the war. She was commandant of the Sandon Red Cross Hospital and had been chairman of the Stone Refugees Committee since 1914.[2] The assiduous work of the rank and file of these various committees was recognised by the regular appearance of their names in the local newspapers, whether as committee members, organisers of fundraising events and socials, or as donors of money, goods in kind and even houses.

Fundraising to support Belgian refugees took many forms in Staffordshire. There were big events like the Patriotic Concert for the Belgian Refugees held in October 1914 at the Victoria Hall, Hanley. Here one could hear the celebrated Belgian pianist Arthur de Greef accompanied by the North Staffordshire Symphony Orchestra. All proceeds were given to the Mayor of Stoke's Belgian Refugee Relief Fund. There were many flag days like that in Newcastle in November 1914, which raised the impressive sum of £114: 'practically every person of every class in every part of the town was reached during the day'. This major exercise was organised like so many fundraising initiatives on the home front by women, in this case led by the mayoress.[3]

Supporting the refugees practically and financially brought new people into the burgeoning voluntarism of the home front. In Stafford, they had quickly formed a Belgian Refugee Committee. Its honorary secretary was Violet Bostock (1892–1961), aged twenty-two at the outbreak of war. She was the daughter of Edwin Bostock, a director of the local family owned shoe firm, and niece of the town's mayor, H. J. Bostock. The diligence of this committee meant that by July 1915 fifty-two refugees had been housed in the town, with a further five in private homes. Thirteen had already left Stafford. The committee continued to collect money for the maintenance of refugees and for those who were still suffering in Belgium.[4] Their fundraising competed with a growing range of wartime causes.

Most voluntary efforts focused on demonstrating practical support for the ordinary 'Tommy'. From the early months of the war, money was raised to make and buy what were called comforts to send to soldiers and sailors, including scarves, cakes and cigarettes. The Tamworth Ladies Working League was one example of the kind of voluntary effort undertaken because of the war. The league was formed to provide for Tamworth men who had volunteered. Its moving force was Mrs Ethel Hamel of Bolehill House whose husband Felix was a leading local figure as a JP and borough councillor. In September 1914 she called a meeting to begin Red Cross work in Glascote when a large number of ladies offered to make garments. Soon, as well as making articles, the league were raising money to buy goods to send to the Red Cross and to the Tamworth Territorials. A musical matinée in December 1914 raised over £30 so that the league could supply plum puddings and 1oz of tobacco to each of the 125 Tamworth Territorials and to the Tamworth home defence men stationed in Essex. By January 1915 they had extended their activities to make garments such as body belts and flannel shirts for all serving Tamworth men. Local officers put in orders for their men such as the fifty pairs of pants requested by Captain Jenkinson of 'C' Company. Soldiers regularly sent thanks and made personal requests, such as for candles so they did not have to sit all night without light. The league sent hundreds of parcels to Tamworth men at the front.[5]

By 1917 the ladies were also running a nightly buffet at Tamworth station for soldiers in transit. Every night an average of 800 cups of tea, coffee or cocoa were served. Hundreds of men were supplied weekly in the waiting room, with cakes and meat pies sold in large numbers. The league raised money not only to make and buy food but also for replacement crockery, often carried away on the trains. They also served refreshments to relatives en route to visit wounded men at military hospitals. At the end of the war, this was seen as exactly the kind of voluntary effort that women who did not need to engage in waged work could give as part of their patriotic contribution. Tamworth's mayor congratulated the ladies on the self-sacrifice they had shown in conducting the buffet. Their efforts carried on beyond the Armistice, as the buffet was still needed and soldiers continued to request socks and shirts.[6]

Supplying comforts to the troops was not just the province of the middle classes. The girls working at John Shannon & Son's factory in Tamworth subscribed among themselves to send a parcel of 1,250 cigarettes to Tamworth Territorials in France. Other women engaged in similar sorts of activities but on a more domestic scale. For sixteen-year-old Lois Turner of Stone doing her bit involved writing much-appreciated letters to soldiers as well as making gloves, scarves, cakes and chocolates, which she sent them at the front together with cigarettes. Sewing groups mushroomed across the county making bandages and all sorts of comforts for the troops. In Walsall a ladies committee was set up quickly, presided over by the mayoress, to coordinate the work of sewing parties throughout the town. The Stafford Red Cross Central Workroom formed in February 1916 in its initial three months made 1,840 articles from pneumonia jackets to swabs. They supplied the needs of local Red Cross hospitals and sent the residue to London to be distributed at home and abroad. In December 1916 a special knitting fortnight in Lichfield produced woollen comforts for Staffordshire troops on active service such as 311 mufflers, 150 pairs of mittens and 91 helmets.[7]

Putting on entertainments was a favourite way to raise money for comforts for the troops. These galvanised people's generosity even as the cost of living kept rising. Col Blizzard transferred his formidable recruitment skills to winning support for Col Blizzard's Comforts Fund for the North Staffordshire Regiment. He organised football matches between Stoke and Port Vale football clubs, as well as between Blizzard's 5th North Staffs XI and an All England XI. The latter raised £650 even before the gates were opened. Over the war, he raised the considerable sum of £5,029 for the comforts of North Staffordshire soldiers. These comforts included footballs, cricket bats and enamelled drinking mugs, particularly

A badge of the 5th North Staffordshire's Comforts Fund.

appreciated because they were easy to keep clean and unbreakable, as well as cocoa for men on duty in exposed positions at night. Many cinemas and halls of the home front often advertised special performances in aid of one fund or another.[8]

Pre-war charitable work was considerably extended to meet the needs of war. From the outset many people were swept up into local relief committees, Red Cross societies, Soldiers' and Sailors' Families Associations (SSFA) as well as existing charities. All turned their attention to ameliorating some of the hardships brought by the war or to providing comforts to serving and wounded soldiers. Walsall SSFA operated through ward committees and raised money through collections at churches, chapels, clubs and patriotic concerts. By December 1914 they had raised £310,318 19s with lists of subscribers printed in local newspapers. By January 1916 this SSFA had registered 2,596 wives, 4,598 children and 1,358 other dependants (including fathers, mothers and unmarried wives), providing grants to them including for funeral expenses. The town also had a separate Prince of Wales Relief Fund to deal with civilian distress.[9]

Looking at the make-up of these local committees, it is striking how many of them drew on the local great and the good, or their wives. The Walsall Workers War Committee complained that the local SSFA 'were people in comfortable and cosy positions, and were not touched by stories of distress of widows and wives of the brave workers who were fighting for their country'. In some cases the figureheads were members of the local aristocracy or gentry. The Earl of Dartmouth (1851–1936) as Lord Lieutenant of Staffordshire, was chairman of the Staffordshire Territorial Force Association. His wife, the Countess of Dartmouth (1849–1929), was the Staffordshire president of the British Red Cross Society and of the Girl Guide Corps for the county. She seems to have opened events and sat on platforms, rather than giving stirring speeches or working behind the scenes as an active committee woman. Their son, Gerald, was killed on active service in 1915.[10]

Another couple show the diligence of many in the voluntary effort that sustained the home front in Staffordshire. Mrs Cornelia Rowland was thirty-seven at the outbreak of war. She had five young children and was part of the servant-keeping classes in Lichfield. In 1911 she and her husband, Dr Frank Rowland, lived in a nineteen-room house with four live-in servants. In October 1914, he transformed their drawing room into a five-bed ward for wounded soldiers. Together with Red Cross nurses, he ran this facility for eighteen months beside his other medical works. From 1916, he was chairman of the Mid-Staffordshire Local Medical War Committee, which arranged a rota of doctors to serve in the Royal Army Medical Corps while making provision for their practices to continue in their absence. Both the Rowlands were assiduous fundraisers for the Red Cross. In a profile of him after the war, when he was awarded a CBE, it was noted that in all his war work Dr Rowlands 'was heartily supported by his wife'. The Lichfield War Hospital Supply Depot, which she founded, supplied around 20,000 garments to wounded soldiers and she organised the first flag day in Lichfield. Indeed, it is her name which is more apparent than his in the Lichfield wartime press. She was part of the committee formed to organise hospitality for Belgian refugees in Lichfield and was particularly active in the local Red Cross Society. She gave around three days a week to this work, which, she said, was all her available time from home duties. She was responsible for all cutting out, packing and secretarial duties at the depot. Of the flag days she organised, it was said 'scarcely anyone to be found in the City who had not got a flag or in many cases two or three flags. Altogether some 10,000 flags were disposed of'. Their first flag day in November 1915 raised over £107, which exceeded all expectations. Mrs Rowland also was a 'zealous chair' of the committee organising a flag day for the North Staffordshire's Comforts Fund, at the request of Col Blizzard. Her voluntary activism in Lichfield increased her profile and she seems to have been a well-known public woman. By 1921 she was president of Lichfield Women's Institute. However, she was not a political woman and declined the invitation to sit on Lichfield's Profiteering Committee in 1919.[11]

Volunteer Red Cross workers in the grounds of a convalescent home for injured soldiers on Stone Road, Eccleshall.

Although Red Cross fundraising occurred right across the county, in some towns there were more localised responses to the new demands of war. One example was the Empire Club, formed at St Chad's Schoolrooms, Tipping Street, Stafford, for members of the forces when they were visiting the town. It opened from 6 to 9.30 p.m. on Saturday and Sunday evenings to cater for the large numbers of soldiers who came into the town from the camps on Cannock Chase. 'The Club is intended to meet the need of a place where soldiers can sit and read, write or play a quiet game, and get refreshments before starting back on their walk to camp'. It opened in June 1917 and seems to have been particularly appreciated by the New Zealand Rifle Brigade (NZRB) stationed at Brocton. To begin with around 130 soldiers attended on Saturday nights, including wounded soldiers from the infirmary, who were entertained with strawberries and cigarettes. Fundraising was undertaken in Stafford, such as a matinée showing at the Picture House of Marie Corelli's 'Temporal Power'. In February 1918 the NZRB Band put on a Grand Khaki Concert at the Picture House with all the proceeds going to the Empire Club. People had to be turned away from the packed event, which took over £26 at the door. Now attendances had risen to 423 and the club was also offering free billets, including supper and breakfast, to soldiers stranded in Stafford. As most of the lady volunteers on the committee had sons in the Army, every effort was made to maintain the 'homely' character of the club, which required more fundraising. Sometimes the Empire Club was the focus of a collection and at other points it was the venue for fundraising for other causes. A sale at The Hough, a large private house in Stafford, was in aid of the Empire Club and the longer-running Welcome Club, a similar facility for soldiers and sailors run in the town's Free Library. In December 1918 the Empire Club was lent by the vicar of St Chad's so that tea could be provided by lady workers of Queen Mary's Needlework

Plaque commemorating the Empire Club, Tipping Street, Stafford.

Guild as part of a matinée fundraiser at the Picture House in aid of the Guild. A party of wounded soldiers from Sandon Hall Red Cross Hospital were brought so that they could enjoy the event.[12]

Families involved themselves in a range of what sometimes seemed a never-ending series of appeals to people's generosity. A wine merchant explained to Stafford Borough Tribunal how his family were doing their bit: two sons were in the Navy, his daughter was secretary to a committee of ladies making bandages for the wounded, his wife managed a soldier's club and he was secretary of the Vegetable Products Committee for the Navy. A draper from Leek making his case to the local tribunal said he was treasurer of the Local National Service Committee and had raised almost £ 70 for the *Weekly Dispatch*'s Tobacco Fund. He also claimed to have raised £ 300 for the Red Cross.[13]

War Savings drives and later Tank Weeks were a way in which whole towns were encouraged to come together to raise significant sums for the prosecution of the war. In 1918 Stafford's 'Boom Week' raised £145,000, well over the target set for them of £67,000 to pay for twenty-seven aeroplanes. The NZRB Band was part of the announced attractions, along with a procession of civic dignitaries who performed a formal opening while an aeroplane flew over the town dropping leaflets. Employees of the various workshops and factories in the town, together with shops and schools, were encouraged to compete to see how much money they could raise. Tank Weeks were organised in the major towns of the county. They were a way to see for oneself these new weapons of war as a real tank was displayed as the focus for crowds to buy war bonds. Wolverhampton's week raised £1,002,499. Everyone could join in small or larger ways. Edith Birchall recorded in her diary, 'We four girls and Mother marched off to invest our Christmas box in tank. Mother has given us £20 to invest in war bonds.'[14]

War Savings Committees worked away even in very small villages. Ellenhall raised £212 for war bonds during Business Men's Week, enough, it was said, to pay for nearly three machine guns. Their success was due to the untiring work of their secretary, Miss Franklin, with special praise given to committee member Miss Hare, the postmistress. More informal fundraising could take many shapes. One example was Wilmot Martin, a farmer at Hixon, who

Vegetables for the Fleet, *Staffordshire Advertiser*, 27 November 1915.

gathered round him all the available musical talent of the neighbourhood and organised what became known as the Hixon Concert Party, consisting chiefly of local farm workers and friends …. [T]hey have visited scores of mid-Staffordshire villages, travelling by means of Mr Martin's own motor, giving an evening concert to raise money for the deserving fund that they were so eager to support.

Over the war the Concert Party collected £1,200 for St Dunstan's Hostel for Blinded Sailors and Soldiers. They used whatever transport they could during the petrol shortages, including driving 14 miles in milk floats in order not to disappoint their waiting audience.[15]

However, raising money was not the only way in which voluntary labour was galvanised in support of the war. Children were encouraged to do their bit. Much of their voluntary contribution to the home front took place through school. Early in the war, St Leonard's School in Bilston revised its needlework curriculum to permit the making of garments suitable for soldiers and their children. Eggs were regularly collected by school children, such as the pupils of Bank House School, Stafford, who in April 1917 were thanked for the handsome gift of 515 eggs that they had sent to the National Egg Collection for the wounded. Many places had stories like this one from Wigginton school. During a recent collection of eggs for wounded soldiers some of the children were allowed to write their names and addresses on them. One bearing the name of Willie Stanford came into the possession of Private William Davies, of the King's Shropshire Light Infantry, at the military hospital in Hampstead. Davies wrote to the boy thanking him:

It is very kind of you and your chums to think of us Tommies. I quite enjoyed the egg. I have been in this hospital six weeks, and two weeks in a French hospital. I have had my leg off, lost it at the battle of Ypres … I am a bit battered about, am I not? But I'm still cheery. I am 18 years of age next October, so I am not much older than you, perhaps.

AEROPLANE BANK WEEK AT LICHFIELD.

Civic dignitaries pictured at Lichfield's Aeroplane Bank Week, *Staffordshire Advertiser*, 23 March 1918.

These stories together with the competition to collect as many eggs as possible were all part of ways in which everyone could be wrapped into the larger patriotic effort. Figures for various collections regularly appeared in the press: 1,524 eggs were collected in April 1918 in Lichfield and district for the National Egg Collection.[16]

Children were also mobilised to maintain the supply of a key wartime commodity – jam. The importance of jam to the war effort was recognised by national drives to collect blackberries in the last years of the war. Jam made stale or adulterated war bread more palatable principally to soldiers but also, where supplies allowed, to those on the home front. In Staffordshire a scheme was created in 1918 where schoolchildren gathered blackberries in 160 collecting depots across the county. This was considered so urgent that others were encouraged to join in. However, there could be unforeseen risks in berry picking. Ten Cannock children went onto the Chase near the Rugeley camp to pick wild bunchberries. They wandered into the camp area and found under a bush what proved to be an unexploded grenade. One of the boys threw it into the air and when it hit the ground it exploded with alarming results, injuring seven of the children, who had to be taken by soldiers to Cannock Hospital.[17]

School log books across the county recorded days given over to blackberry picking and other war-inspired foraging. The log book of Kinver Boys' County Primary School shows an energetic response from schoolchildren doing their bit. Chestnuts and acorns were requested by the munitions industry, but it did not always go to plan. In January 1918 the head complained that the twenty sacks of horse chestnuts collected by the boys in the autumn had still not been collected despite repeated requests to the Ministry of Munitions. The

Public Notices.

NATIONAL EGG COLLECTION FUND.

WHITE HEATHER DAY

Will be held at UTTOXETER, on WEDNESDAY, September 29.

In Aid of National Egg Collection for our Wounded Soldiers and Sailors.

Don't Forget to Call on the Local Palmist at her Stand in Lloyd's Bank-passage, Carter-street. You will be Interested and Amused.

All Proceeds on this day will be Spent in Buying Eggs for the Wounded.

An advert for one of many events held in aid of the National Egg Collection Fund, *Staffordshire Advertiser*, 25 September 1915.

chestnuts were deteriorating rapidly, so in the end he had to arrange for a carrier himself. The sacks finally left the school on 25 January 1918. The school then joined in the nationwide blackberry picking that was heavily promoted in autumn 1918 to make jam for the troops. An average of thirty boys went on each foraging trip. Nineteen hundredweight of fruit was collected and forwarded to a jam factory in West Bromwich.[18]

The biggest reservoir of untapped voluntary labour was women, and some men, who could afford to forego a wage. They were recruited to the Voluntary Aid Detachments and were known as VADs. All over the county people came together to create new Red Cross Auxilary hospitals, staffed by voluntary labour. One example was Freeford Hall offered to Lichfield Red Cross Society by Major and Mrs Dyott, which opened in October 1914, initially to nurse wounded Belgian soldiers. Bedding and equipment was given or loaned by friends and neighbours. Throughout its lifetime the Freeford VAD hospital was staffed by two VAD detachments who gave wholehearted service quite voluntarily. At its close in January 1919 it was said of the VADs, 'No praise can be too high for their ungrudging and cheerful work.' The Lady Superintendent, Mrs Daisy Stuart Shaw, trained the VADs and organised the nursing section of the hospital. Her husband was one of the two doctors who constituted the honorary medical staff and he also gave voluntarily 'invaluable service, most patriotically and unselfishly'. Mrs Shaw's VAD card shows that in addition to her work at Freeford, she also gave unpaid time as head of the swab room at the War Hospital Supply Depot in Lichfield when her other duties allowed. She was to be elected as Lichfield's first woman councillor in 1919. The photo used to illustrate her pioneering achievement shows her in her VAD uniform. She and her husband were some of many Staffordshire citizens who as members of the servanted class, did their bit by working voluntarily and energetically fundraising for many causes while coping with the anxiety of a son serving at the front. Their only son, Lieutenant R. R. S. Shaw, was killed in action on 1 July 1916, aged twenty.[19]

GNOSALL RURAL DISTRICT.

WAR AGRICULTURAL SUB-COMMITTEE.

BLACKBERRY COLLECTION.

Owing to the Shortage of Fruit this year, the Ministry of Food are relying upon the BLACKBERRY CROP TO PROVIDE JAM for His Majesty's Forces and the Civilian population, and at their request arrangements are being made in Staffordshire for Harvesting the Crop by Gangs of Pickers acting under Supervision of School Teachers and Local Volunteers.

My Committee therefore Appeal to Owners and Occupiers of Land

1.—To refrain from Brushing Hedges until after the Blackberries are gathered.

2.—To grant facilities to authorized Pickers to enter on their Lands to gather the Blackberries.

The Pickers will be instructed to do as little damage as possible, and the Supervisors will do all they can to prevent unnecessary trespass and damage.

H. G. A. SMITH, Secretary.
Newport, Salop, 14th August, 1918.

Organising the collection of blackberries in Gnossall, *Staffordshire Advertiser*, 17 August 1918.

Staffordshire provided many VADs. One was Christine Stewart, daughter of a member of Uttoxeter Urban Council, who died of pneumonia while working as a nurse. She was one of eight children of a butcher. She was twenty-three when she died towards the end of 1918 in Stourbridge. It was said of her, 'When the Roll of Honour came to be made of those in the town who had died in the service of their country, Miss Christine Stewart would be included as having sacrificed her life in the same good cause.' A high-profile Staffordshire VAD was Florence Thorneycroft (1869–1944) of Tettenhall Towers, Wolverhampton. She was

NEW WOMEN COUNCILLORS IN STAFFORDSHIRE

MRS. SOUTH
(Stafford).

MRS. SHAW
(Lichfield).

MISS FARMER
(Longton).

Above: The first women councillors elected
in Staffordshire, including Mrs Stuart
Shaw in her VAD uniform, *Staffordshire
Advertiser*, 9 November 1919.

Right: Florence Thorneycroft in her Red
Cross uniform, 1917.

Commandant of the VAD Hospital Tettenhall from when it opened in 1915 until 1919. That
year she was welcomed to Staffordshire County Council as their first 'lady member'. Less
well known at the time was the only woman on a Staffordshire war memorial, Annie Allen
(1872–1919) of Eccleshall. She was the daughter of the local vicar, educated privately at
home, who assisted with parochial work when her health permitted. She volunteered at the
military convalescent hospital run by Sandon & Eccleshall Red Cross, rising to be one of the
two quartermasters at the hospital. She died of a sudden attack of laryngitis in January 1919
and at her funeral there was an honour guard of VAD nurses. The bond between VADs could

Four WAACs at Rugeley camp, 1917.

last. When Winifred South died from double pneumonia aged twenty-nine at her home in Stafford in 1925, it was noted that she had been a VAD at the local Infirmary and a significant number of her VAD detachment attended her funeral. Winifred's unpaid labour had included night work and meeting convoys of wounded soldiers as they arrived at Stafford railway station. She served from 1915 to beyond the end of the war.[20]

Some Staffordshire women served overseas as VADs. A contingent of fifty nurses left for the front in May 1915, including six Staffordshire 'ladies'. One was Miss Nora Wright, daughter of Col C. H. Wright JP of Tillington Hall, Stafford. Her background, typical of many volunteers, explains her ability to offer her services as a VAD. Another volunteer was Dr Agnes Porter who, since 1913, had been one of the Staffordshire Education Committee's assistant medical inspectors. She was volunteering as a bacteriologist for the Scottish Women's Hospital Unit in Serbia when it was captured by the Austrians in early 1916.[21]

There were other appeals for women to volunteer. At a WAAC recruiting meeting in Newcastle in March 1918, the mayor appealed to women to enrol in the Women's Army so that men might be released for the fighting line. Afterwards they would be proud to think they had done their bit. It was explained that WAACs could not only release fit men for the war front, but they could enable skilled tradesmen and craftsmen to return to civilian life and thus keep industry going. At the same meeting Lady Balfour said she felt

voluntary work was characteristic of our country, and, therefore, the WAAC would prove immensely valuable … The appeal was not to the men now; they had gone. The call was to the women; would they be slow to do their bit? She thought not, because the hearts of the women were every bit as true as those of the men.

The WAAC was organised into four units: cookery, mechanical, clerical and miscellaneous. WAACs contributed to the running of the military camps on the Chase, for example by working in canteens.[22]

It was in a similar spirit that Staffordshire women were asked to volunteer for the Women's Land Army. Lord Dartmouth led an appeal in the county to contribute to the 30,000 women recruits that the Board of Agriculture called for in April 1918 a little more than a year after the WLA was formed. A large number of mobile workers were needed to cultivate newly ploughed land in order to maintain food supplies. The targets were women and girls from the towns who were not already engaged in war work. They were needed to take the place of men who had to go to France or to replace the Home Defence Forces men sent abroad. There had already been a rally of Women Land Workers at Borough Hall, Stafford, on 29 January 1918 with a procession through the town. There was applause as the first of the 150 women and girls wearing 'the characteristic and business-like' costume of the WLA 'took up the step of the military march played by the band of the New Zealand Rifle Brigade. The music was appropriate. It was entitled "The Great Little Army"'. WLA selection committees operated at Stafford, Wolverhampton, Stoke, Burton and Leek. Despite 743 applicants in early 1918 only 25 per cent were accepted as meeting the required standard of character and physique. At the end of January there were eighty-four Staffordshire girls working in the county with a further sixty-nine elsewhere. They had an enormous symbolic value and their numbers did grow. However, even combined with rural women already working on or returning to the land, they were never going to solve the wartime food crisis. However, the rallies continued. In Stafford in May the aim was to recruit 1,000 Staffordshire girls who were urged to 'let the Germans see what material Englishwomen are made of'. Sixty women stepped up to volunteer. In Uttoxeter in June 1918, women were told that the need was so great that they could join for as little as six months and they were reassured that there was now no prejudice towards women

Women's Land Army parade, Stafford. Their banners read 'The Nation's Food' and 'God Save the King', 1919.

Portrait of Baron Hatherton, *c.* 1900.

working on farms. The WLA was gradually demobilised at the end of the war but not finally disbanded in Staffordshire until November 1919 after the potato harvest. The work of these women was not unpaid, but was governed by the Agricultural Wages Board, although the language used was of volunteers freeing up men for military service.[23]

The other major manpower requirement of the war was peopling the huge number of committees that grew up to enable the home front to function. Almost invariably it was men who were turned to, although not all were the middle-class and even aristocratic figures who had long run Staffordshire's civic organisations. Lord Hatherton (1842–1930), a significant local landowner, was already extraordinarily active before the war as chairman of the Quarter Sessions, of the County Council and of Cannock Board of Guardians as well as presiding magistrate at Penkridge. However when the Military Service Tribunals were assembled in 1916 (the year of his seventy-fourth birthday), he took a key role in Cannock Rural Tribunal and his comments are often to be found in the Mid-Staffordshire Appeals papers. A rather different kind of public man equally involved in running the home front was Councillor Henry Simmons (1857–1920) of Stafford. He was a long-standing trade unionist in the local boot and shoe industry. He felt one of his wartime achievements was to have increased the membership of the Stafford branch of the Boot and Shoe Operatives including women workers. He claimed that the outstanding feature of his work in the boot trade was to win a minimum wage, which had led to the doubling of women's wages to 23s. However, his activism was not confined to trade unionism. He had served on the town council for a good many years, specialising in the housing of the working classes. Aside from participating in various council committees, in the war he added service on the Borough Tribunal, the Food Control Committee (FCC) and the War Savings Association. Like Lord Hatherton, Simmons had two sons serving in the Army.[24]

The other group who were prominent in the new structures of the home front were existing public servants. Eustace Joy was the leading example in Staffordshire. He was the county's leading official as clerk to the County Council. His position meant that he played a key role in putting the county on a war footing, participating in meetings of the Staffordshire Territorial Force Association and supporting the organisation of the National Relief Fund in the county. Through the opening years of the war, Joy appeared in the press speaking at or doing the administrative work for organisations set up in response to the emergency. He also found time to organise a Red Cross concert in Stafford in February 1916, but from that year his energies were directed to managing Staffordshire's manpower through being a military/national service representative at the tribunals of mid-Staffordshire and a tireless secretary of the county War Agriculture Committee. In May 1918 he resigned from what he called the honorary position of military/national service representative. He regretted that this 'would entail the abolition of the very carefully constructed machinery for investigating cases which had been built up during such period'. He remained an energetic administrator of all the schemes for which the WAC was responsible.[25]

The various local tribunals and official committees generated by the war consisted almost entirely of men, who were not salaried or waged but who might receive expenses. This limited who could afford to take on such tasks, and therefore who had the power to adjudicate on what might be matters of life or death, or at least which men had to go into the Army. When the tribunals were set up to judge appeals for exemption under the Military Service Act, the Local Government Board suggested that they should include representatives of local Chambers of Commerce, 'a fair proportion ... should be representatives of labour' and that 'women may be placed on tribunals with advantage'. In Staffordshire no women were selected for this role, but when it came to FCCs set up in the summer of 1917, at least one member had to be a woman. As people in authority looked around for others to populate the growing number of committees required across wartime Staffordshire, they turned to the other men they knew and then to their wives and families. This tended to reinforce local hierarchies and to some, such as the Walsall Workers War Emergency Committee, this was 'class favouritism'.[26] The war did not really change the access of people to the spaces in which the local home front was created and sustained, except at the margins.

This was a space seized, or stumbled into, by some women even in a conservative county like Staffordshire. Wartime voluntary work was often crucial to this transition. Ellen South (Mrs C. F. South) (1867–1948) was married to a well-known auctioneer who was secretary of the Staffordshire Chamber of Agriculture. She was an active volunteer in wartime carrying on her existing charitable commitments such as to the local NSPCC as well as contributing to patriotic activities such as organising and performing in the pageant, A Masque of Empire, in aid of the Red Cross in 1915. In 1916 she began a collection of wastepaper with the help of boy scouts and many women volunteers in Stafford, which stretched out into the wider district until curtailed by petrol shortages. In fifteen months she and her voluntary helpers collected 39 tons of paper, raising over £132 for a wide range of local wartime funds. Her activities on the home front drew her into networks with other active women such as Violet Bostock on Stafford Belgian Refugee Committee and the women who together would form Stafford Women's Citizen Association. This made her the kind of publicly known woman who was turned to when women were needed on wartime committees. She was a member of Stafford's FCC and the anti-profiteering committee. This placed her in a good position to be one of the WCA's two candidates for Stafford Town Council in 1919 when the considerably extended female local government electorate could vote for the first time. Stafford was the only place in the county where this new women's organisation stood candidates. She was elected as the town's first woman councillor and was immediately appointed chairman of the Maternity and Child Welfare Committee. In 1921 she was again a pioneer, becoming one of the borough's first women magistrates together with two other women, Mrs Annie Dix and Miss McCrea, who in their different ways had also been active participants on the local home front.[27]

Unlike Mrs South, Annie Dix (1869–1963) was a working-class woman aged forty-five at the outbreak of war. She was already active before 1914 but the war increased her opportunities to influence decisions that affected daily life in Stafford. She was the wife of a railwayman who was secretary of Stafford National Union of Railwaymen and mother of three children, the youngest being ten in 1914. She was the founding president of Stafford Railway Women's Guild, as well as a member of Stafford Guild of Social Welfare and a Poor Law Guardian. On the home front she added membership of the FCC, including the Communal Kitchen Committee, and the War Pensions Committee. She helped set up the Women's Section of the Labour Party in Stafford and then in 1921 was appointed as a magistrate. She may well have known another unusual civic woman on the Staffordshire home front – Mrs Charles Adams (always named in this way) of Walsall. When the Walsall Trades Council formed a Food Vigilance Committee in June 1917, Mrs Charles Adams was appointed as its secretary. She was a vocal spokeswoman for it throughout its life, in person and in print. Her badgering of the local FCC on behalf of the local working class led to her being added to its membership in March 1918. She also spoke at a local meeting to mobilise new women voters on behalf of Labour, which was reported as 'Women and Democracy. Home System which wants "Smashing to Atoms"'. Another better-known example was Emma Sproson, elected as Wolverhampton's first woman councillor in 1921, who was active in pursuit of women's suffrage before the war through the Women's Freedom League. On the home front she was a noisy advocate for the working class on Wolverhampton FCC.[28]

Whatever the scale of their voluntary work including the many hours of labour by VADs, WLA members and WAACs, most volunteers undertook tasks that did not challenge the sexual division of labour. There was men's and women's work for volunteers just as much as there was for those in waged work. However, the huge increase in voluntary work during the war created new experiences for some women: an independent identity and the acquisition of new skills and contacts, which widened possibilities for some when peace came. The home front could not have been sustained without significant levels of voluntary labour. Whether by donating to many wartime funds, organising local flag days or entertainments, or giving unpaid time to the vast number of committees and activities generated by the home front, Staffordshire men, women and children did their bit.

CHAPTER FIVE

EVERYDAY LIFE HAS TO GO ON

Daily life on the Staffordshire home front was affected by growing shortages of food and fuel as well as price increases for everyday necessities, but the impact on individuals varied across the county as the war dragged on.

The cost of living rose quickly. This picture of Leek in January 1915 gives a flavour of what that meant for ordinary people:

A short time ago, a loaf of bread could be bought for 5d in Leek ... and now it is 7d ... a family of eight (and the average number of children in the poor family ... is six) would take about six quartern loaves a week. ... Meat of course is dearer... But fish is extravagantly dear... The bloater has become a luxury ... and plaice is at a prohibitive price as far as the poor are concerned. Eggs are altogether out of the question, and margarine has to take the place of butter... coal is unreasonably dear. ... House rents have also increased, and for anything like a decent working man's dwelling six shillings a week rent will have to be paid. ... But we never knew the Leek trade to be so flourishing, especially in winter, or wages to be so high as they are now; so there is a silver lining to the black war cloud that is overshadowing us.[1]

However, silver linings were not apparent everywhere in the county. For the first years of the war, the key was whether household incomes could keep pace with rising prices. In the latter years of the war although the cost of living kept rising, the problem of shortages became particularly acute.

Food

By November 1916 the *Staffordshire Advertiser* despaired at the lack of government action on 'The Food Problem'. They noted the scarcity of basic foods and the continuous rise in prices, which together were inflicting great hardship on the poorer classes, causing discontent. The paper was openly critical of the 'tardy action of our rather nerveless Government ... [who] have delayed taking the obvious course until it was too late to render real and practical assistance'. The suggestions already being made by the government for voluntary food economy were, it thought, 'fatuous': 'It is worse than fatuous for so-called food economists to suggest meatless days when in countless homes already no meat has been tasted for weeks together.' Reflecting the shift in public opinion, the paper took the view that 'If any real economy in consumption is to be brought about, it will have to be by some form of compulsion, each family being allowed a certain amount of food according to the mouths to be fed'.[2] In the end this would come to pass, but there was still two more years of the home front to come.

Food shortages became most severe in Staffordshire from 1917. Early in the year potatoes, a key staple of the working-class diet, had become scarce: in February the supply of potatoes in Hanley was said to be unequal to demand. The government had created a

Food economy posters were everywhere. They can be seen behind a group of volunteer nurses outside Borough Hall, Stafford.

Ministry of Food in December 1916 led by the first Food Controller, Lord Devonport. His decision to set maximum prices for particular foodstuffs was meant to ensure that the necessities of life were not priced out of the reach of ordinary people. However, price fixing could not prevent shortages and, in some cases, exacerbated the situation. Potato shortages meant that Staffordshire shoppers could be found queuing at 6 a.m. in the hope of securing some of the limited supply. In March 1917, in Wolverhampton 'the market was practically clear of potatoes. At one stall a queue of women was regulated by the police'. As a consequence, as a columnist in the *Staffordshire Advertiser* noted in April, 'potatoless days are a matter of course ... meatless days are common, and sugarless days are not unknown'.[3]

Food economy campaigns began across the county. All the local newspapers published a letter from the Lord Lieutenant of Staffordshire on 'The Food Crisis', which explained why personal action was now vital:

It is a war of the people, a war in which we can all, old and young, man and woman, play our part or take our share ...

Lord Devonport is the official head of food control, but the real food controller is the mistress of the house, whether it is a large one or a small one – she it is who can and ought to stop waste, she it is who can and ought to limit the rations.

The mass of the population must have bread; to the poor it is the chief necessity of life. The rich and well-to-do can afford to buy other things; the poor cannot – their need is the greater, their requirements should be our first consideration. ...

We all profess to be willing to do our 'bit' to-day, and if in doing our own 'bit' we can do a 'bit' more for those who want it most, even if it involves a 'bit' less for ourselves, then indeed will our own 'bit' have a double value.[4]

However, the situation did not improve.

By mid-1917 the average price of food was double that of 1914. The success of the German U-boats in sinking merchant shipping was producing real shortages in a country so dependent on imported foods. One solution was to grow more produce. This could be undertaken at different scales from the industrial to the domestic. However, local action – ploughing up a significant acreage of grassland by often reluctant local farmers and the creation of allotments in Staffordshire's towns and villages – could not by itself solve the problem. As the crisis deepened in the summer of 1917 a new initiative was taken to address the increasing tension. Each local authority had to set up a Food Control Committee (FCC) to safeguard the interests of consumers, rather than producers or retailers. FCCs had many responsibilities, which grew as the food crisis intensified. These included tackling waste, enforcing the ministry's mushrooming numbers of food orders including prosecuting food hoarders, as well as trying to find a fairer means to share meagre resources whether through collective provision such as communal kitchens or by implementing the first ever food rationing in the country. Particular districts experienced the food crisis in different ways but for much of the war they had to create their own solutions, choosing which of the nationwide initiatives for food economy and food control to implement in ways that would have the support of local people. The food crisis had brought home to the public and politicians alike that shopping for necessities, the cooking and sharing of food within families, and the management of household resources were no longer private matters. What food was eaten, who got the lion's share, how well the food was cooked and how much was wasted had until this point been largely private choices. What was new in wartime was the idea that the state could at first advise and then directly interfere in private decisions within all households. What did not change was that whatever else the war economy demanded of her, it was a woman's principal task to keep the household going.

By autumn 1917, for many the only way to ensure your family got basic food stuffs was to join the new phenomena of the home front – the food queue. These became a reality for many in Staffordshire in the winter of 1917/18. Earlier in the year they were reported with some humour, as this limerick printed in the *Leek Times* shows:

> Little Miss Muffet got many a buffet
> Waiting for 'spuds' in a queue,
> After ten weary hours
> In twelve April showers
> She got half a pound and the 'flu'.

Later in the year there seemed less to smile about. The editor of the *Leek Times* described a local food queue:

Whilst writing this, both roadway and pathway opposite the Maypole [a grocers] are blocked by a crowd, consisting chiefly of women and children, standing in the slush and snow, shivering in the cold, waiting to get served. It is painful to see the old people pushed about and crushed in the pressure and the pinched faces of the young. The chief things wanted are tea, margarine and butter; and it is quite time that some way of distribution was adopted that would avoid this scandal.

In Stoke it was said, 'Many of the people in the food queues were food hogs who were getting more than their share by going from one shop to another, and the shopkeeper had not the power to refuse to sell.'[5]

Some thought the queues were necessary to bring home to people how serious the country's situation was. The chairman of Stoke FCC argued that the queues

STAFFORD

Industrial Co-operative Society, Ld.

Important to Members.

SUGAR SCHEME.

Dear Sir or Madam,

Have you returned your

DECLARATION FORMS

to us yet ? If not, please do so at once as

The Distribution

by our new

Food Card System

commences on

Monday, Dec. 24th, 1917.

Members who are not registered with us for Sugar may obtain Food Cards from their usual trading branch.

per pro THE COMMITTEE,

J. R. HOLMES LAIDLER, General Manager.

A message to Stafford Co-op members about the new sugar cards, *Staffordshire Advertiser*, 22 December 1917.

had not been altogether an unmitigated evil. … He was satisfied that a great many people had not realized that position, and that they had been doing little in the way of practicing economy. The queues had brought it home to them beyond doubt that there was a real shortage, and for that reason they had done good, although they caused inconvenience.

His FCC decided to ration tea and margarine from early February 1918 in the hope that this would reduce the queues. However, he warned that shortages of meat, bacon and cheese would be acute for some time to come. There would continue to be a need for great

LICHFIELD RURAL DISTRICT.

FOOD CONTROL COMMITTEE.

Notice is hereby given, that after MONDAY, the 25th February, 1918, NO BUTCHER in the LICHFIELD RURAL DISTRICT WILL SELL MEAT to anyone but his REGISTERED CUS-TOMERS (except in the case of Sailors and Soldiers on leave).

All Persons wishing to be Registered should take their Ration Card for Tea and Butter to their Butcher at the earliest opportunity, who will endorse it and enter their Names on his list of Customers.

THOMAS MOSELEY,
Executive Officer.
6, Breadmarket-street, Lichfield.
14th February, 1918.

Lichfield Rural District Food Control Committee introduces meat rationing, *Staffordshire Advertiser*, 16 February 1918.

economy. People were urged to do all they could to find substitute foods to replace those that were short.[6]

In early February 1918 the *Tamworth Herald* still noted local queues but said they were occurring in other towns too, despite local rationing schemes. Until there was a national scheme, they argued, there would be queues. Blame was apportioned: some thought shopkeepers were slow in serving customers whereas in Walsall it was said 'some women liked standing in queues'. For others the cause was people's greed: 'It seemed to be the idea of some people to get all they possibly could regardless of others.' A demonstration in Smethwick in January 1918 showed many feared that the cause of the problem was profiteering and only national control of all foodstuffs with equal rations for rich and poor would end the queues and the hardship.[7] In the meantime the first step to ration scarce goods took place locally in FCC districts.

The food crisis was not solved by the spring of 1918: there were still hardships to come on the home front. However, the range of strategies from voluntary food economy and domestic food production to full-scale compulsory rationing of particular foods was beginning to reassure the public that some kind of grip was being taken on what was recognised as a dangerous situation. Morale could be so easily undermined and war weariness at home could jeopardise the war front. This was not a new idea.

In September 1917, the *Staffordshire Advertiser* exhorted local people on the home front to 'rise above war-weariness':

As the call for economy is repeated, we must find more things we can do without. Very many of us are nowhere near our limit yet. ... What has been done, and what is to be done still, cannot achieve its full result without the cooperation of those who stand in lines which are far enough from the front trenches, but which are nevertheless part of the actual battlefield.[8]

At this point local authorities through their FCCs felt impelled to speed up national plans for rationing by devising their own schemes to ensure a fairer distribution of resources to banish the queues. At stake was not just that food queues might become food riots and worse, but that as part of a wider war-weariness civilian morale would be undermined, which could lead to the collapse of the home front. It really was the case that, as a wartime poster had it, 'The Kitchen is the Key to Victory'.

Rationing in many ways saved the home front but it had to be invented as this was its first use in Britain. In the summer of 1917 a proposal came from Staffordshire that prefigured the key element in what was to become the British form of food rationing. The Rugeley Food Economy Committee wrote to the Food Controller recommending that the nation's depleted supply of sugar should be allocated to each district proportionate to the number of its inhabitants. The local authority could then place this sugar in the hands of tradesmen according to the wishes of consumers. This would, they believed, prevent the unscrupulous from obtaining sugar at two, three or even four shops.[9] This anticipated the form that rationing would eventually take – with individual consumers registered with a specific retailer for each rationed food.

Another innovation in the mechanics of rationing was said to come from Staffordshire. By May 1918 people were being warned that the present series of food coupons were to

Stafford Corporation
Gas and Electricity Department.

NOTICE TO CONSUMERS.

In view of the very heavy demand for Gas and Electricity for Munition Works, and their use being greatly increased for industrial and domestic purposes, it is IMPERATIVE, in order that URGENT MUNITION WORK should not be stopped, that every CONSUMER should immediately, and for the next few weeks, exercise the greatest possible economy in the USE OF GAS AND ELECTRICITY. IF EVERY CONSUMER will discontinue all waste, they will confer a mutual benefit, viz., to themselves a SAVING in their bill, and to the Department A SAVING OF COAL supplies, of which at present we are extremely short.

Those short of House Coal can obtain supplies of Coke from the Gas Works.

W. M. VALON.

Economy in the use of gas and electricity urged by Stafford Corporation Gas & Electricity Department, *Staffordshire Advertiser*, 12 January 1918.

come to an end in July, when a book of coupons would be issued with leaves of different colours to denote the various articles rationed. The scheme was to be applied to the whole of the county and would, it was claimed, simplify the first system of loose cards. This arrangement was based on the suggestion of Revd Harold Smith of Tixall, from his experience as interviewing officer for Stafford Rural FCC. The continuing success of rationing depended upon careful organisation. In Walsall 90,000 books were issued for the new ration scheme in July 1918. It was reported that meat supplies were now satisfactory in the town and that it was hoped to be able to continue to provide two-thirds of the ration as English meat but everyone would have to take their share of frozen meat. Flour supplies were now plentiful but that was not the case for milk, as yield had fallen off by about a half and unless rain came, the outlook was reported to be gloomy. As a result, it was announced there was no prospect of a better cheese supply for the moment.[10] The implementation of a national compulsory scheme of food rationing did not end the food crisis but met a popular demand for an equality of sacrifice, where meagre resources were to be fairly shared irrespective of one's income or social status. But the pressures did not relent. The Armistice did not put an end to the need to economise and to ration food and fuel. Wartime regulations continued to apply into peacetime and organising the winding down of food control took some time.

Fuel

Intimately connected to the food crisis on the home front was the growing shortage of fuel. This affected heating the home but also the ability to cook whatever food the housewife was able to acquire. Like food, fuel had been an issue at the beginning of the war. Just as there was panic buying of food in early August 1914, there was also a 'silly panic' in the demand for coal.[11] 'Silly', so the readers of the *Cannock Advertiser* were told, because the coal previously exported to Germany and other parts of Europe would now be thrown onto the domestic market. Yet the war did affect the cost and availability of household fuel, with the competing demands of the military and the war industries leaving the requirements of the home far behind. Moreover, like food there was no direct intervention in domestic consumption of coal on the home front for the first years of the war. As with food, there were issues concerning price, the effect of labour shortages and the distribution of scarce resources.

In the small village of Hints, it was noted in the school log book in March 1917: 'We have been without coal all week, only what has been borrowed – and the weather is still cold.' Two days later, 'Still no coal – school closed this afternoon – several children away – deep snow'. The distribution of coal was becoming an increasing problem. Messrs Samuel Barlow (Tamworth) Ltd announced that with regret, owing to the scarcity of labour, they were unable to continue to deliver coal by bags, although they would continue to supply coal in loads. The Retail Coal Prices Order, 1917, gave powers to local authorities to set prices for coal and soon their detail was publicised so that everyone knew the maximum chargeable in their district. In some cases, as in the extensive list published by Cannock RDC, distinctions were made between different types of fuel: Good House Coal, Medium or Best House Nuts or Kitchen Coal. Prices also took into account the distance coal had to be transported from wharf, colliery or shop.[12] This was to try to control access to a limited resource.

In the summer of 1918, the fuel crisis became acute in Staffordshire. In May, Uttoxeter RDC was told that owing to the conscription of 10,000 miners, and to the increased requirements of the government, there would be a diminished coal supply during the war and for some time afterwards. It would therefore be necessary to appoint a local committee

Fuel shortages begin to appear in adverts, *Staffordshire Advertiser*, 29 December 1917.

to ration the supply. In July, the citizens of Walsall were told that coal supplies from the area that had been used to supply the town were now to be diverted to London. As a consequence, no one could forecast whether there would be sufficient coal for the coming winter. As with other rationing, there was an enormous amount of technical detail that the customer as well as the retailer needed to be aware of. A ninety-five-page Coal Order was received in Lichfield and was due to come into operation at the end of July 1918. The fuel

The cost of fuel shortages to the housewife, *Staffordshire Advertiser*, 25 May 1918.

allowance (coal or coke) was based on occupied rooms ranging from 3½ tons for two rooms to 12 tons for twelve rooms. There was also an allowance of gas for lighting, which was also based on room occupancy. As fuel became rationed, pilfering coal began to surface as a crime in local police courts. In October 1918, a boatee was charged with stealing coal. He had thrown four pieces of coal off his canal boat into George Whitehouse's garden in return for garden produce and flowers. Although the value of the coal was only 1s 6d, both men were fined £5 each.[13] As we will see, some of the solutions proposed to the food crisis were also designed to deal with the effects of fuel shortage. The Ministry of Food was particular keen that local FCCs explore whether creating communal kitchens might be the optimum way to share scarce food and fuel.

Daily life

Living through Staffordshire's wartime food and fuel crisis affected local people in different ways. Members of families or neighbours could have different experiences from one another, while fissures appeared between urban and rural communities as tensions increased among farmers, retailers and consumers.

The Tunstall diarist Edith Birchall was in her early twenties during the war. She does not appear to have had any responsibility for the preparation of meals, yet she had to eat like everyone else. It is therefore striking that in her wartime diary food features primarily in terms of going out for tea rather than noting the more mundane and unrelenting tasks associated with feeding herself or her household. She enjoyed teas out in London, Birmingham and Cardiff as well as at home in Staffordshire (such as at Biddulph Old Hall) and even had lunch in the dining car when returning from college. In 1917 she noted that by January 1918 they would have sugar ration cards but made no other references to rationing. There is no sense of food queues or biting shortages; the only one she recounts is the dearth of matches in October 1918, which affected her new habit of smoking.[14] Then suddenly that month she decided to record in detail what the war had meant to food prices. This stark reminder of the huge rise in

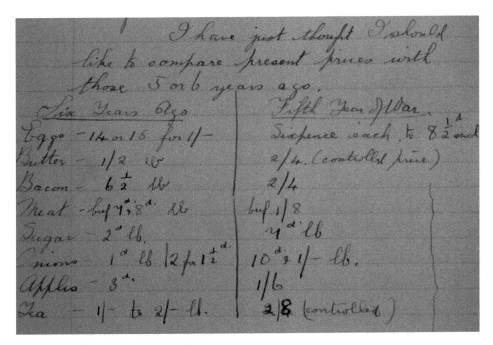

Edith Birchall's diary, 1 October 1918.

the cost of living over the war years shows that a young working woman, still living at home, did know what was happening to the prices of necessities and that many were now subject to controlled prices. At the same time she was able to conduct her work, social and family life without complaining the inconveniences of the home front.

Edith's experience was not universal. For some, the war created new anxieties about how their families were to survive. When Mrs Rose wrote to Eustace Joy in February 1918, she revealed the desperate challenge faced by one ordinary Staffordshire family. Mrs Rose described how she coped looking after her disabled daughter (aged twenty-one but with a mental age of ten) without the financial support she had got from her miner son who had recently joined the Army. He had previously earned as much as £2 a week, which, she claimed, would have increased now that he was twenty years old. However, her household now had to survive without this money. She also had a sixteen-year-old son whose ill health meant he had had to give up working underground, which had considerably reduced his contribution to the household. Moreover, her own work was not permanent. All this uncertainty was exacerbated by the

cost of living being so high I feel very depressed under the condition of things; then again my daughter is an enormous eater and does not understand the scarcity of money to obtain it. … If I was alone, only myself to care for, I would not mind. I would have been nursing in France or anywhere I could have done my bit, but as you know, my children to me come first of all.[15]

She said it was eight weeks since her son had enlisted and she had gone short 35s a week. She hoped that Joy as a military representative might be able to get her son released from the Army. Others also 'Worried about Food', as the headline to a report of a Walsall inquest the same month put it. The case was of a twenty-six-year-old miner's wife whose body had been found in the canal. She had gone out to buy bottled milk but never returned. She was found with ration cards in her pocket. Her husband said that his wife had been troubled because she could not get as much food as she wanted. He had told her not to worry and not to stand in queues, as he would put up with anything. He had noticed her getting thin and a little nervous but her only worry had been about food. Nevertheless, the verdict was suicide.[16] Between these extremes were all sorts of ways in which individuals on the home front dealt on a daily basis with the local effects of the developing food and fuel crises. The war affected how one shopped, cooked and ate food.

Shopping

The challenge of daily shopping changed over the war as prices increased, shortages grew, shops had to close, queuing became necessary and then finally the shopper had to navigate local and then national systems of rationing. Growing number of wartime regulations meant that the quality of goods on sale often deteriorated or they became harder to find. The conditions of everyday shopping changed over the war but also varied from town to town and between rural and urban areas. However, the biggest issue for any shopper was how to balance the various demands on the household income (itself often unpredictable) to provide an adequate diet for the family while meeting all the other household costs such as rent, fuel and clothing.

Increasingly, the time everyday shopping took and the distances travelled in pursuit of food were to put very real pressures on those who were usually responsible – the housewives. Even the idea of how rationing would work in practice could cause anxiety. A woman in one of the remote villages of the Tamworth district asked in early 1918,

S. R. Lovatt's

PROVISION STORES

WILL BE

CLOSED

MONDAY, TUESDAY, WEDNESDAY,

AUGUST 5th, 6th, 7th.

Customers who usually buy their Butter, Margarine, and Lard on these days will be permitted by the Food Committee to purchase them

To-day (Saturday).

Arrangements to get rationed goods over the bank holiday, *Staffordshire Advertiser*, 3 August 1918.

Are we really going to be able to obtain under the rationing order in quality and quantity from the little village grocer's shop, if we have registered there, those stores that we have been in the habit of tramping lately, miles upon miles, to obtain from the larger town stores?

It was explained to her that the whole point of the Rationing Order was that 'she should be able to obtain at the village shop the supplies of the rationed articles she had hitherto had to walk to Tamworth to secure'. However, it was conceded that it would take a little time to work smoothly.[17]

As food became short, shopkeepers introduced their own ways to distribute scarce goods. They were said to favour particular customers. Some grocers refused to sell sugar to a shopper unless tea was bought at the same time, until the Sugar Commission (charged with regulating the wartime sugar supply) forbade it. Walsall Food Vigilance Committee, formed by the local labour movement, protested at the practice of shopkeepers, especially butchers, of serving favoured customers at the back door. The local FCC gave instructions that manual workers should have the first claim on meat. However, just being able to get to shops was an issue for some women war workers, particularly those who worked in munitions as they left home early and did not return until late. They had no time to join the queues. Some tradesmen opened earlier to meet their needs but then there were queues all day.[18] The problem was that some shoppers who had the time and the means chased supplies and lower prices across wide distances. In order to thwart this, some adjoining FCCs equalised the prices of key commodities across the whole area. All of these issues made shopping more of a challenge for everyone. How far should one travel to find queues to join or was queuing pointless if some people could jump the queue?

Even when attempts were finally made to share out scarce resources and to try to regularise prices within a locality, there still needed to be shops or markets where food could be bought.

Spencer's shop, Weston, showing their delivery cart, *c.* 1914.

Opening hours of shops was a concern throughout the war. Each district came to its own arrangements. By September 1916 Tamworth shops closed earlier than before the war: on Mondays, Tuesdays and Thursdays at 7 p.m., Wednesdays at 1 p.m., Fridays at 8 p.m. and Saturdays at 9 p.m. This was because of lighting restrictions 'as well as the fact that the shops now employ many girl and women assistants, who are not so well able as men to undergo long hours of labour'.[19]

As the range of shops available in particular neighbourhoods began to change, this affected the experience of shopping on the home front. The grocery trade was affected like other businesses by men joining the Army. Cases before the Mid-Staffordshire Appeals Tribunal show how the war affected the provision of shops in rural and urban areas. The grocer in Cresswell, Stoke-on-Trent, showed in his case in 1916 that this was the only shop in the village. He had built up a delivery round over the five years he had owned the shop: 'I have to take these things to them if I must keep their custom.' He also acted as an agent for a local farmer, selling on to the public all his butter and eggs. Despite his detailed account of this

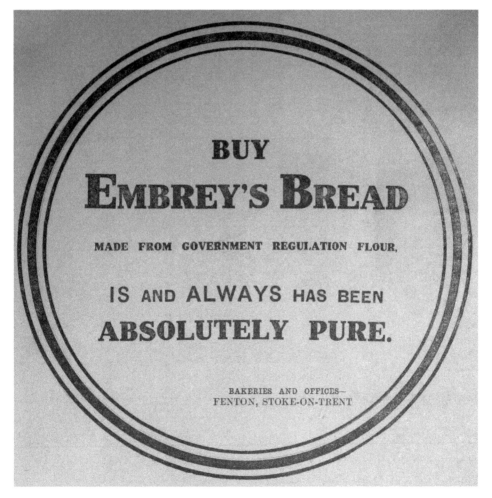

A baker advertises bread made with unadulterated flour, *Staffordshire Advertiser*, 26 May 1917.

busy little shop and why he was necessary to it – 'My wife cannot handle sacks of corn and sides of bacon, and other great weights' – the local tribunal 'thought that the wife could very conveniently attend to the small grocery business'.[20] Decisions of a local tribunal could mean a village would lose its only shop and those in the countryside no longer get deliveries. This put considerable strain on those running small shops.

In the towns there were similar effects. When the Appeals case of the manager of one of the Stafford branches of the London Central Meat Co. was heard in September 1916, the company said that the loss of labour had already forced the closure of two of their four branches in the town (and ninety branches across the country). Their claim that the loss of this man would mean the closure of another butcher's shop in Stafford was not accepted by the military representative. He suggested the company had already made the same claim for another store yet it had not closed despite the enlistment of its manager. Many towns had branches of local Co-operative Societies: Stafford Co-op had eight shops in and around the town while in February 1918, it was claimed that the Co-op catered for a fifth of the population of Walsall. Like other businesses they had to adapt to the loss of men to the Army. In 1916 the Rugeley Co-op had a trade of £40,000 a year and employed a manager and nine staff. They had replaced enlisted men '(to our limit) by female labour to conduct our business successfully and only employed men who had attested or had been rejected for army service'.[21]

The issue for the shopper on the home front was that not only might long-standing shops become vulnerable to closure or limit their services, but also the staff working there were likely to be less experienced. Labour shortages in shops demanded changes of behaviour from the shopper, as the Leek Traders' Association warned in June 1915:

Of the shops in Leek most of them are totally without male assistants, while the staff of others are seriously depleted. Practically all the assistants' places are being kept open for them and owing to the serious shortage of labour it is almost impossible to obtain messenger boys. Therefore under these circumstances the employers appeal to the shopping public to cooperate with them in the patriotic efforts they are making by complying with the following suggestions –

1. Carry home purchases as far as possible.
2. Send weekly orders for foodstuffs in writing in order to save time in copying out those given verbally.
3. Shop as early as possible and do not expect immediate service during busy hours.
4. And they would also suggest that if small purchases were paid for at the time much labour would be saved in book-keeping.[22]

Particularly after the introduction of conscription in 1916 the face on the other side of the counter might well be female or a man whose age or health debarred him (at least at this point in the war) from military service. Some of the larger employers negotiated the loss of staff with the tribunal, substituting male workers who had received a low medical grade or even women for the men who had been conscripted. A number of the multiples like the Home & Colonial Stores made the point that they had not employed any female assistants before the war but now, across the company, they employed over 2,200 women in order to release fit men. John Salmon's grocery and provision store in Market Place, Cannock, also had only one male employee at the end of 1917 (he had curvature of the spine). Seven female assistants were now employed at the store, which in turn supplied two branch shops. The change in who staffed local shops was sufficiently noticeable that in a review of the local experience of the home front in 1917 across the county, it was noted of Uttoxeter that women 'have invaded many shops … where previously only male labour was employed'.[23]

Consumers were also served who lived some distance from retailers. Some businesses sold directly from farms such as William Holdcroft of Rose Cottage Farm, Barlaston. In 1916, he had 100 customers in Trentham and Fenton to whom he delivered milk, vegetables and eggs. Bread deliveries seem to have been a common service. In the appeal of a Tamworth baker, it was reported that after he had done a day's work in the bakehouse he then delivered from 400 to 600 loaves. Hartley Boon of Sandon Road, Stafford, advertised his good nourishing bread and it was noted 'You will see his van on its delivery round' not only supplying bread but also groceries.[24] The conscription of delivery men affected these services.

Shops even had to close because of the loss of staff and/or the owner to the Army. It was not unusual to see adverts such as the one for a butcher's business in Little Haywood. The owner had been called up for military service and was selling the only shop within a wide area. He claimed he was the only butcher between Stafford and Rugeley, supplying meat to all of Colwich, Great and Little Haywood, Ingestre and Milford. He told his tribunal, 'if I go all these districts will ... be without a meat supply'. A tribunal in 1917 heard that there were now only three bakers in Tamworth for a population of 8,000. Sometimes local tribunals would disagree about how many bakers or butchers a community required. In the case of George Upton, a Rugeley butcher, the appeal tribunal suggested in February 1918 that as there was now only half of the usual supply of meat available, there was no need to keep a butcher in the district who was of military age. The local tribunal disagreed saying that the only other local butcher of military age was known to have as much work as he could manage. These decisions affected where one could shop.[25]

The shopper experienced pressure on how and where she shopped and on the amount and quality of goods she purchased. Initially it was suggested that the best way to deal with shortages and rising prices was for everyone to limit their consumption voluntarily. Local papers carried the Food Controller's advice that every adult should restrict themselves to 4lbs of bread, 2½lbs of meat and ¾lb of sugar per week. Quickly advice became regulation when it came to the most important staple in the diet – bread. In March 1917 the Food Controller issued a number of restrictions on the sale of bread, the breaking of which meant the offender could be prosecuted under the Defence of the Realm Act. Local newspapers busily spread the word so that shoppers, bakers and grocers understood the implications for them. Bread had to be twelve hours old before it could be offered for sale, it had to be sold to specific weights (1, 2 or 4 lbs) and only in the shape of a tin loaf, no sugar could be added to it and currant, sultana or milk bread could no longer be offered for sale.[26]

These pressures on the wartime shopper were exacerbated by the fact that even if goods could be obtained their quality might be in doubt. Adulteration could be unofficial (and therefore criminal) but it could also be officially sanctioned. In January 1917, a farmer in Stretton in the east of the county was fined the large sum of £30 for adulterating milk with 19 per cent added water. The prosecution said rather emotively, 'He must have known that a quantity would ultimately reach Burton Infirmary, where wounded soldiers were being treated.' Sometimes the issue for food was substitution rather than adulteration. Walsall FCC discussed whether to allow the sale of horsemeat. They did not want horse to be substituted for other forms of meat so they ruled that, if sold, it must be limited to separate shops.[27]

However, one officially sanctioned adulteration was that made to bread. Staffordshire residents were warned in November 1916 that a form of 'war bread' was to be instituted. Flour was not to be ground so fine and could be adulterated with other grains and even potatoes. The Bread Order, 1917, formed part of the drive for food economy. The idea of only permitting the sale of twelve-hour-old bread was that stale bread was less palatable

FOOD CHANGES

are liable at first to cause inconvenience and discomfort to many people who are not blessed with a first-class digestion. It is well therefore for all such persons to be upon their guard and to adopt precautionary measures until the digestive system is able to adjust itself to the changed conditions of diet. A little suitable medicine at such a time is, in fact, a necessity, and for the purpose Beecham's Pills are to be recommended. These famous pills have a world-wide reputation as a digestive medicine. They have a tonic influence upon the stomach, a corrective action upon the liver and a cleansing effect upon the bowels. If these organs of the digestive system are kept in thorough working order people will have little to fear from changes of diet. It is certainly well for everyone to fortify the digestion in these days by taking

BEECHAM'S PILLS

Dealing with the effects of the wartime diet: an advert for Beecham's pills, *Staffordshire Advertiser*, 25 August 1917.

and therefore unlikely to be squandered. Quickly prosecutions occurred across Staffordshire, often to draw attention to the new regulation. In Hanley the case against two bakers revealed a strategy adopted by some to meet the requirements of the Bread Order. These defendants said they weighed the bread before it left the shop and if a loaf was found to be deficient the weight was made up by cutting off a piece from another loaf. The Chief Inspector of Weights and Measures for Stoke-on-Trent told the court that this practice was unacceptable to the Food Controller who thought bakers should be able to cut dough to reach the right weight when it was baked. The bakers said that twelve-hour-old bread shrank and lost weight once it came out of the oven.[28] The challenges of the Bread Orders were significant for the baker and the shopkeeper but also were confusing for the shopper.

Although the issue of the weight and relative staleness of a loaf concerned the shopper, most complaints were about its palatability. War bread was thought to cause digestive troubles: the Ministry of Food recommended, 'Eat no more than you really need, and chew every mouthful slowly and well', to which a piece in the *Staffordshire Advertiser* added the advice that the best way to cope with war bread was to take a half teaspoon of pure bisurated magnesia in a little water after every meal. But the bread was to get worse before it got any better. At the end of 1918 a case was reported in Stone where in the course of a prosecution for selling bread that was not twelve hours old, the baker complained of the bad flour with which he had been supplied. As a result of using it, 300 loaves had been returned because people refused to eat them. He claimed that the Bread Order was responsible for more waste than any order that he knew.[29] Because the Bread Orders (the 1917 order was reissued in 1918) were applied and policed beyond the end of the war, bread was never rationed unlike in other countries. The housewife could shop around for bread and, it seems, even return it if it was inedible. However, with the introduction of rationing that was not possible for other key elements in the daily diet.

The pattern established with sugar cards, the first form of rationing, was eventually the model for the national system of compulsory rationing, which was gradually rolled out across the country through 1918. In the interval many local authorities devised their own systems of rationing, particularly for fats, tea and meat. The goods covered in these local systems varied as did the amount and price of rationed goods. However, what most forms of rationing did was to tie the shopper to a particular shop, which was the only place where their card or coupon could be used. This affected daily shopping, and may also have benefitted the grocers over the specialist provision dealers, as the shopper might choose to buy the non-rationed goods she required from the same stores that held her ration card. Just knowing whether and where you could buy particular foods and what price you might be expected to pay provided a challenge to everyday shopping, which in turn disturbed pre-war habits. As the home front developed in Staffordshire, shopping for a household's daily diet took up more time and demanded more flexibility in terms of what was bought and where.

There were other ways of acquiring food other than shopping. One way was to grow at least some of it, either by acquiring one of the new allotments created in response to the food crisis or just growing vegetables in the garden if one had one. There was advice on dealing with surplus produce with demonstrations of techniques to preserve fruit and vegetables. If some made jam (for which they had to apply for an additional ration of sugar) or preserved vegetables so they could be used out of season, others took more desperate measures. As the food crisis deepened, all sorts of foodstuffs became valuable enough to steal. In February 1917 two miners from Tamworth were charged with stealing swedes from a field. They wheeled away their spoils, valued at 1s 6d, on a handcart. They were sentenced to fourteen days hard labour. One robbery at Audley consisted of tubers taken from six drills, which were 26 yards in length. Poachers of rabbits also came before the courts, such as two men caught with bulging pockets and carrying rabbits along with a net and 150 yards of driving line that had been recently used. The more experienced poacher (he had twenty-seven convictions) was fined £5 while the other was fined £3, and the net and line were confiscated.[30] However, the theft of food or stealing to buy food remained a fairly rare occurrence on the Staffordshire home front.

More common was buying directly from farmers or engaging in a little animal husbandry. Local rationing schemes did not prevent buying butter direct from farmers if they were still making it. The only condition was that for each sale, the card of the consumer had to be marked by the farmer or the person delivering the butter. If anyone obtained more than the allotted quantity in any week, or the person supplying failed to mark the card, then they were both liable to be prosecuted under DORA . Others kept animals, although that was not always straightforward. A protest meeting was held at Wolverhampton in the late summer of 1918 because, it was said, working men had been encouraged to buy pigs but now they could not get sufficient food for them. The amount allowed by the authorities was barely sufficient to keep the pigs alive. One said that he had seen some pigs running about that were 'more like greyhounds than pigs'.[31]

The war saw increasing efforts to persuade women to grow and preserve fruit and vegetables and to keep animals such as rabbits and poultry. To encourage this, the government promoted the establishment of local organisations for rural women following the successful example of the Canadian Farm Women's Institutes. These were the Women's Institutes (WI). Mrs Clews from the Board of Agriculture's WI Department told a public meeting in Uttoxeter, 'Women were asked to meet and learn how to do various garden work, preserve fruit and vegetables, the good cooking of foods, and in these and other ways it was found that women could assist very materially in the present crisis and make themselves efficient.' Among the practical sessions at Staffordshire WIs during the war were ones on bread making, rug making, soft toy making, 'making over' adults clothing into children's, war cookery, fruit bottling and canning as well as lectures on pig and poultry feeding. Many of these skills were focused on creating goods for sale to bring in much-needed money for its women members rather than on encouraging self-sufficiency in rural villages. There was a varied response to the campaign to encourage the formation of WIs in Staffordshire. A successful early WI at Gnossall regularly reported its activities in the press, but other parts of the county did not always respond with such enthusiasm. A meeting held just after the Armistice with the hope of forming a WI in Colwich only had a 'meagre attendance'.[32]

Keeping pigs or hens, growing vegetables and fruit, foraging and even poaching or stealing were never going to be the main way in which Staffordshire people fed themselves, but for some wartime revived skills or encouraged the acquisition of new ones, whether for growing or poaching. However, acquiring the ingredients for a meal was only the beginning of daily survival on the home front.

Cooking

As the price and availability of particular foods limited the possibility of tried-and-tested recipes, the press provided hints on how to economise and stretch expensive food such as meat into a family meal. However, these recipes presumed the time to cook in a more challenging way and that the recipients would accept changes to their daily diet.

Stimulated by the first campaigns of the new national Ministry of Food, local initiatives provided guidance on preparing and cooking scarce foods and avoiding waste. The focus was on persuading civilians to cut their food consumption, particularly of bread. The housewife in her kitchen was seen to be central to this campaign, which took the form of food economy exhibitions, wartime recipe books and cookery demonstrations and lectures as well as

One way to cope with the expense and scarcity of foods was to use substitutes, in this case for eggs, *Staffordshire Advertiser*, 25 May 1918.

posters urging 'The Woman who Wastes a Crust, Wastes a Bullet' and 'Break the Bread Habit: Remember Others have the Same Right to Live as You'.[33]

Throughout the summer of 1917, lectures were given across the county advising on how best to cook given the increasing challenges of the home front. Practical demonstrations could draw substantial audiences. A session on cooking economically at the Corporation Street Girls' School in Stafford attracted 150 mothers. The audience bought the 500 scones and cakes of oat, barley and maize that had been prepared by the schoolgirls, and asked for a further demonstration on making bread from wheat substitutes. Villages and smaller towns were not to be left out: a series of demonstrations on the most economical ways to prepare meals from wheat substitutes were given in King's Bromley, and they also discussed whether to club together to buy particular foods or to start cooperative jam making. However, not all these initiatives were popular or effective: in Eccleshall, it was felt that the cookery demonstrations had not been a success and it was decided not to attempt them again. Instead, they decided to focus on emulating Stone's provision of inexpensive dinners to school children as they felt this would be a way of saving on cereal foods.[34]

The means used to cook was an issue for voluntary and compulsory curbs on the consumption of food on the home front. This became even more pressing as fuel shortages began to take effect. Readers of the *Cannock Advertiser* were given a number of suggestions about how they could decrease their consumption of coal – consider how many fires you can do without; cook fewer hot meals; reduce the number of hot baths – as well as ways of 'stretching' coal by mixing it with coke, putting fire bricks in grates where possible and making sure that all kettles and saucepans were free of soot. The importance of these small acts was made clear to those far from the fighting: 'Remember that every pound of coal saved helps to keep our soldiers warm, and assists our French, Italian and American comrades to beat the Hun.' Earlier proposals to use hayboxes to save fuel never got very far. In June 1915 a demonstration of 'the art of the hay-box or fireless cookery' was given in Stafford. The fifty mothers who attended heard how this simple contrivance could reduce the cost of fuel by up to 60 per cent. The *Staffordshire Advertiser* also provided instructions on how to make a similar haybox out of a Tate sugar box.[35] Although other displays were occasionally reported across the county, the haybox did not have a wide appeal. Soon both the time and the hay needed to operate the haybox were in short supply.

Food and fuel economy came together in the discussion of communal kitchens, one of the innovations of the home front. One of their advantages was that this was a way to cook for large numbers while saving coal. However, the idea of a communal kitchen was contentious in many places.

Eating Together

Communal kitchens were often discussed in Staffordshire as part of the push for food economy in 1917, but with varying results. In Wolverhampton the local Labour Representation Committee campaigned for a communal kitchen from July 1917. However, translating this demand into action took time. A National Kitchen and Restaurant was eventually planned for the YMCA buildings in Darlington Street at an estimated cost of £965. It opened in early 1919. Beside the kitchen was a restaurant that could accommodate eighty diners and an outdoor (takeaway) department. The facilities were the height of modernity: electric fans kept the atmosphere pure in the restaurant while the cooking equipment was operated by gas and electricity.[36]

In Lichfield discussions went on for almost as long but with a different outcome. The local FCC set up a committee to research national kitchens. The Ministry of Food was keen that every district should give the proposal serious consideration. It argued that the advantages lay in economy of food and fuel; the supply of nutritious and well-cooked food at reasonable prices on a self-supporting but not profit-making basis; the substitution of skilfully prepared and properly cooked wholesome meals for makeshift meals; and the economy of labour achieved by the collective preparation of food. The committee included one woman, Emily Pinder, who was quickly convinced of the case for a Lichfield communal kitchen after her visit to Cannock's. This was open five days a week, served everything in penny portions and was staffed mainly by volunteers. It had been started six months earlier because of the coal crisis and was designed to feed children 'for whom there was an absolute need'. It was run separately from the local FCC, made a slight profit and planned to widen its provision to the general public during the coming winter. The Lichfield committee was told in September 1918 that a communal kitchen was necessary even at this stage of the war for 'even if the war was over ... the food difficulties would probably be worse than at the present time'. It was anticipated that one of the conditions of the peace would be that Britain would have to divert food coming into the country to feed the starving populations of Germany and Austria. It was therefore still important to start communal kitchens all over Britain. The FCC recommended that the council start such a kitchen in Lichfield. Importantly, 'it would not be on a class basis but would be open to everybody, rich or poor, without distinction of any kind' and could be set up with an interest-free loan from the Local Government Board. Those who argued for a Lichfield communal kitchen urged swift action because of growing coal shortages, which would make it difficult for everyone to get sufficient hot meals during the approaching winter. One said,

even if it does cost the rates something I think it is a war measure we ought to carry out. It would tend to relieve the difficulties of many who, as war workers or for other reasons connected with the war, have little time for the preparation of food.

Despite these arguments and the support of the mayor, the caution of other councillors won out. Lichfield did not get a communal kitchen.[37]

Gladys Harvey (standing) and Ada Potter worked in the canteen at Brocton camp.

Other parts of the county did not hesitate. Walsall was proud that they were early in the game: they opened a communal kitchen in June 1917 as part of their pre-FCC food economy activities. In the Potteries there were various national kitchens. The Longton kitchen and restaurant, opened in September 1918, could seat 150 and served takeaway meals. The reasonably priced menu varied each day and was arranged so that no coupons were necessary.[38] The latter was an important issue for potential customers.

In rural areas the idea of a communal kitchen got shorter shrift. When Uttoxeter RDC received the circular from the Food Controller urging the creation of national kitchens, they were unwilling to act; it was not considered to be of any advantage in a country place. Other villages were less cautious, such as the mining village of Cheslyn Hay. They had decided in May 1917 to start a communal kitchen and later claimed to be the first village in England to have done so. By the end of that year they announced that it had provided 6,264 meals over the previous eight weeks. The kitchen (always called a communal rather than a national kitchen) ran for eighteen months and never ran into debt. It was their success that persuaded Chadsmoor to also open a communal kitchen. It first served meals in March 1918. By early May the kitchen was providing an average of 220 meals a day, which, it was hoped, would soon rise to 800 daily meals.[39]

Communal kitchens were not the only form of collective eating on the Staffordshire home front. Canteens were another wartime innovation in some workplaces. One example was Siemens Canteen, Stafford, which advertised for a capable cook in July 1918. The introduction of local rationing highlighted the extent to which certain workers could add to their rations by receiving meat meals in their works canteen as well as sharing in the general meat ration at home. Walsall FCC asked whether this was fair. A member of the local Trades Council argued, 'All workpeople have not got canteens, and [a national kitchen] would be the means of putting a substantial meal within the reach of those who need it.'[40]

Wartime did not mean that opportunities to eat out in cafes and restaurants diminished, although the experience might change. The German waiter, a well-known phenomenon before the war, rapidly disappeared from the home front either because he left the country at the outbreak of hostilities or because he was interned with other enemy aliens. Among the thirteen German prisoners taken from Stoke in September 1914 for detention in Lancaster were the chef and head waiter at the North Stafford Hotel, Stoke.[41] Waitresses were increasingly employed instead of waiters.

Restaurants and tearooms were started to meet the new needs of the home front. The Wolverhampton YWCA included a restaurant as they felt this was 'one of the best ways of helping the girl life of a town or city, especially when so many women and girls were working harder than ever'. In March 1915 a Tipperary Room was opened in Walsall, one of fifty across the country. Its purpose was to provide a centre where the wives and mothers of men serving in the forces could meet for friendship and recreation with cheaply priced light refreshments. After a year, they had 689 members and had added another kind of communal provision. From March the caretaker opened the rooms at 6 a.m. so that girl munition workers could get hot tea, coffee or cocoa before going to work. Across July 1917, this facility attracted over 3,000 women.[42]

Other refreshment rooms were commercial ventures. One of the Mid-Staffordshire Appeals cases centred on James Hitchener, a refreshment-housekeeper at Penkridge Bank. His premises were carefully situated halfway between Rugeley and Rugeley Military Camp and served 2,000 soldiers per week as well as the general public. However, Lichfield Rural Tribunal felt that the refreshment room was not a necessity and Hitchener could be spared to join the Army. Meanwhile, adverts in the press reveal other cafés and restaurants. Many and changing delights of Turner & Co, General Drapers and Ladies Outfitters, were advertised each week of the war in a large advert in the *Staffordshire Advertiser*. From June 1916 it was announced that the store now had its own tearooms.[43]

Together, the communal/national kitchens and restaurants, canteens, refreshment rooms, and cafés of the home front provided ways for people to get cooked meals outside the home. There were economies of scale to be made through these facilities as well as saving on the scarce resources of food and fuel. Most importantly for daily life on the home front, they also took a little pressure off the women (housewives and servants) who otherwise had to find a way to translate whatever food they had managed to acquire into nutritious and edible meals.

Far from the guns, the war affected the ordinary tasks of daily life for Staffordshire people, particularly getting, cooking and eating food. The experience of living on the home front changed over the war years but in time the increasing cost of living and shortages of basic foods and fuel began to affect everyone. All were asked to do their bit by economising but in the end the introduction of local and then national rationing designed to share scare resources helped to ensure the survival of the embattled home front.

CHAPTER SIX

DIFFERENT EXPERIENCES ON THE LOCAL HOME FRONT: THE STRANGERS

The Staffordshire home front was experienced differently depending on where you lived, how the war affected your household income and how you coped with unrelenting anxiety about male family and friends who were at the front or who might be conscripted into the Army. One way to learn a little more about the diversity of experience on this home front and how it changed over the war years is to consider how the war shaped the lives of various groups who, for one reason or another, were regarded as outsiders. They can be grouped together as enemy aliens or friendly foreigners or troublesome locals. This chapter highlights some of the experiences of strangers resident in the county during the war and the responses of local communities to them.

Enemy Aliens

The home front was constructed in Staffordshire, as elsewhere in Britain, by creating a sense that everyone – whatever their differences before the war – now had a shared enemy. As the war developed the county found different ways to respond to revelations of the presence of Germans in their midst or, as importantly, to panics about hidden enemy aliens who it was feared were spying on unsuspecting Britons or unfairly competing with British businesses or workers. In Staffordshire there were a range of responses to this 'enemy' on the home front from the violent and intolerant to those who refused to see individual Germans as the enemy.

The outbreak of war quickly affected Germans who were working in Staffordshire. The *Leek Post* noted that, 'In comparison with large towns and cities Leek finds employment for a large number of Germans, and as loyal sons of the Fatherland they responded to the call to arms, and left last week to join the German Army.' However, there were anxieties about a hidden 'enemy', fed by newspaper reports about spies in England. In October the *Staffordshire Advertiser* told its readers how twenty Germans had been arrested as spies at the outbreak of war, destroying their spy organisation in England, while nearly 200 more were being kept under observation. Around 9,000 Germans of military age were being held as civilian prisoners of war in detention camps across the country. Some called for even harsher action against Germans still living in Staffordshire. A recruitment meeting in Stafford cheered the radical right-wing politician Lord Charles Beresford when he said,

ACTION FOR LIBEL.

J. LYONS & CO., Limited (Plaintiffs)

v.

LIPTON, Limited (Defendants).

IN the HIGH COURT OF JUSTICE Mr. Justice Sankey, on September 8th, 1914, granted an Interim Injunction restraining Lipton Limited, their Agents and Servants, from speaking or publishing or writing and publishing any words to the effect or of the substance that J. Lyons & Co., Limited, or the Directorate thereof, is composed of Germans, and that by purchasing their commodities the public is assisting the enemies of Great Britain.

J. LYONS & CO., Ltd. (By Appointment to His Majesty the King)

IS AN

ALL-BRITISH COMPANY

WITH

ALL-BRITISH DIRECTORS,

HAS 14,000

ALL-BRITISH SHAREHOLDERS,

AND 160,000

ALL-BRITISH SHOPKEEPERS

SELLING

LYONS' TEA

Cadby Hall,
Kensington, London, W.

A notice announcing a libel case restraining Lipton's from claiming that buying Lyon's tea was assisting the enemy, *Staffordshire Advertiser*, 12 September 1914.

the safety of the realm was of more importance than the flabby sentimentality of a certain number of people who might be inconvenienced by being interned during the war ... The public must see to it that under no circumstances should we risk any harm from the alien enemies amongst us.

In this climate, it is not surprising that the first Germans arrested in the county were assumed to be spies. Four men were arrested in North Staffordshire (three from Burslem, one from Hanley). They were taken to Lichfield where 'their passage through the City in a large motor Black Maria created some little excitement and speculation. After a night in the guard room at Whittington [Barracks], they were again removed but their definite destination is unknown'.[1]

In this atmosphere a number of long-term residents felt they had to establish that they were not German, as was being claimed. At stake were their livelihoods. Notices like this began to appear in local newspapers in September 1914:

Whereas certain evilly disposed persons have circulated the report that I Walter Gask of 182 Watling Street, Bridgtown is a German, I hereby give notice that I am a natural born patriotic Englishman and that my father, mother and all forebears are also English. I believe in FAIR competition, the well-known quality of my meat is maintained. PLEASE GIVE ME A TRIAL. Warning – legal proceedings will be taken against slanderers.[2]

Gask's anxieties reflected the extent that everyday xenophobia had quickly been wrapped into local expressions of patriotism.

There were no long-established German communities of any size in Staffordshire, but there were Germans or people of German extraction scattered through local neighbourhoods working at particular trades such as hairdressing. Some anti-German feeling was apparent. George Giles, secretary of Walsall Trades Council, asserted at the local May Day rally in 1915:

it was possible that the German spy system had something to do with the high cost of living ... If one could get to the bottom of this question, one would find that spies had as much to do with it as anyone else. There were ... 40,000 enemy aliens still at liberty; at the beginning of the war there were 50,000, and only 8,000 had been put into safe places. Those who were responsible for the increased cost of food were hindering the successful prosecution of the war, causing the deaths of the soldiers; and that night's meeting was there to make a big protest against this.[3]

Giles spoke before the Germans sank the *Lusitania* on 7 May 1915, which prompted outbreaks of anti-German violence across the country. Local reporting focused initially on Staffordshire victims: 'five or six homes in the Potteries have been thrown into mourning by the latest and biggest outrage of the Huns'. Many local victims and survivors were members of families who had emigrated to the United States or Canada for work and were travelling to Staffordshire to visit family. One was G. P. Meaney returning from his work in West Virginia to Wolstanton to be reunited with his wife. He had written before he left:

I have booked my passage and given up my job. While you are reading this letter I shall be on the stormy ocean, skipping out of the way of these submarines. Don't worry, for I don't think they will get me. I am going on the fastest boat I can get, so if there is a chance to run out of the way I shall be able to do it ... The Germans have not sunk a passenger vessel yet. And I don't think they will, for they are too well guarded for that ... Well, I am going to risk my neck, anyhow.

Sadly, his optimism was not well founded, and his body was buried far from Staffordshire in Queenstown, Ireland. Among the missing were local men employed on the ship, such as Edward Jones from Shelton who was a member of the ship's orchestra. There were also

POTTERIES VICTIMS OF THE LUSITANIA.

MR. G. P. MEANEY.   WINIFRED BARKER.   MR. JOHN WALKER.

Photographs of some of the Potteries victims of the *Lusitania*, *Staffordshire Advertiser*, 15 May 1915.

victims with connections to Tamworth and survivors returning to Burton and Rugeley. This was shocking enough. It brought the war directly onto the local home front. This was compounded by reports that despite worldwide condemnation, 'In Germany, the dominant feeling is one of exultation.'[4]

The initial riots in Liverpool and Salford against people of German or Austrian birth did not touch Staffordshire. Then the *Tamworth Herald* reported on Saturday 15 May that the prime minister had announced that all Germans not naturalised would be interned and all Germans over military age would be repatriated. The paper commented that many of these people are inoffensive and that this action was probably as much for their own safety as to obviate any mischief.[5] The 'mischief' came to the town that evening.

A dense crowd, reported as numbering 4,000, assembled in George Street, Tamworth, outside Messrs J. Wehrle and Co., watchmakers and jewellers, whose proprietor, Lambert Wehrle, was German. The crowd began to grow from 8 p.m. and within three quarters of an hour more than 200 soldiers had been brought to the scene. Windows were broken in the shop and the rooms above. At intervals the crowd sang snatches of patriotic songs, and indulged in rough horseplay. Towards midnight the crowd began to disperse and by 1 a.m. the streets were practically clear. No arrests were made, and there was no looting of the premises.[6]

Responses to these unusual events varied. The next day at a large recruitment rally in the town, the mayor referred to the disorder in George Street. He regretted the action of a few the previous night. Such conduct would not do any good either for the country or the town, which would have to bear the expense. He thought it would have been better if the young men kicking up a disturbance had been wearing the King's uniform and were going to fight the Germans. Another speaker claimed that there were still men in Tamworth who ought not to be there. Reminding the audience of what had prompted the unruliness, 'If we failed to win this war, England would go down as swiftly and as irretrievably as the *Lusitania* went into the waters of the Atlantic'. Some of the rhetoric hit home, as about forty men gave their names to recruiting officers.[7]

It took a letter from a local soldier at the front to make the strongest protest against the crowd's actions. 'A Tamworth Citizen' said he had come across an account of the attack on Mr Wehrle's shop. He asked, 'What has he done – of what is he guilty?' He said he did not speak from love of the German race but from the Englishman's motto, 'fair play is good sport'. He thought he spoke for all Tamworth men who were his comrades when he asked of the unruly crowd:

Were they able-bodied Englishmen, if so, is it their duty to attack the personality and the premises of an unarmed and harmless citizen, or is it their duty to come out here and fill the gaps in the ranks where their own companions have fallen? Tell them there are Germans out here by the thousand who have to be attacked day and night … Will there be such a crowd outside the recruiting office as there was outside Mr Wehrle's shop? I doubt it … The men out here are ashamed and disgusted at the conduct of their fellow townspeople in so far forgetting themselves.

Lambert Wehrle felt he had to write to the *Tamworth Herald* explaining 'that I utterly condemn all inhuman methods of warfare, especially the use of poisonous gas, and ill-treating and killing of peaceful civilians especially women and children whether on land or sea German men to my sorrow have committed'. Talking of the attack on his shop, 'which all right-minded people have condemned, let me say that I place all my trust and hope in all honourable and God-fearing Britons, that no further useless raid on my premises may take place'. However, the following week's paper reported, 'Removal of Enemy Aliens from Tamworth'. On Monday morning Lambert Wehrle, Franz Bernard Kemper and Johann Klass were removed from Tamworth to a concentration camp in the North of England. It was noted that they were the only male enemy aliens in Tamworth and district.[8]

These names (albeit occasionally misspelled) would not have been new to the readers of the *Tamworth Herald*, and their familiarity may explain how the George Street shop came to be targeted. In March that year a case at the local police court was reported under the headline 'Alien Residents at Tamworth'. The case revolved around Emma and Johann Kuss. She was accused of failing to register as an alien enemy resident. She had only recently moved into the area from Kent, and was now living at Mr Kemper's house in Fazeley. Asked if she was a Russian, it became clear that she was born in Ashford to English parents but her husband was German. She had come to Tamworth with her five children; the youngest was only two months old. Her husband had been interned the previous October but when he was released from the Isle of Man detention camp he had come to live in Tamworth. He had been a British resident since 1891 and was at present working at No. 10a George Street – the premises and home of Mr Wehrle, also a German. Mrs Wehrle was Mr Kuss's sister and like Mr Wehrle, Kuss was a watchmaker. It was suggested that the Kusses' registration was not up to date and that Kemper and Wehrle should have told them what they needed to do when they came to Tamworth. In the course of the press report the names, situation and addresses of all these aliens were published. The Kusses were each fined and together bound over for the sum of £10, their surety being Mr Wehrle.[9] After the sinking of the *Lusitania* it was these three men and Wehrle's jeweller's shop that became the focus for threats.

What this case and Tamworth's anti-German disturbances reveal are another set of home front experiences, that of long-term resident German men and their English wives and children in an increasing culture of hostility. All these men had been living in England for some time. Lambert Wehrle had been a British subject since 1899. His wife was born in Germany, but all but their eldest child had been born in Tamworth. Their youngest child would have been eight at the time of the anti-German disturbances. The family were likely to have experienced directly the threat of the large and noisy crowd as they shared the shop's address. This remained the family home well beyond the war, as in 1939 their son William, also a watchmaker, was living at the same address with his wife. We know more about the Wehrle family as William was conscripted and his case went to the Mid-Staffordshire Appeals Tribunal. The nineteen-year-old watchmaker explained to the tribunal that after his father was interned he was left to carry on the business with his mother. Three sisters and one brother were dependent on them. He explained that the jeweller's shop required a man, first of all for the work and secondly for opening the shop as the old-fashioned shutters were too heavy for a woman to lift. He argued that they could not get a man to take his place (at least not in a few days) as all those they knew had either joined the Army or expected to be called up soon. He had offered his services to the military in March 1916, but was rejected. However, later that year he had to make his case to the Tamworth Tribunal, which was dismissed on 18 May. His appeal against his exemption of a month to arrange the family's affairs was then rejected two days later. So from May 1916 the remaining Wehrle family would have had to cope not only with their father's internment but also with the loss of William to the Army. And it seems they did. William's sisters continued to go to school and one, Ida, appeared in the paper a number of times when she passed her piano exams. Mrs Wehrle's name also appears as a subscriber to a number of funds for soldiers' comforts and for a memorial window.[10]

Somehow or other life went on for the remaining Wehrles in Tamworth. Many wives of interned men found it hard to manage. In November 1915 the case of a wife of a German internee was considered by the Cannock Guardians. Mrs Schiffer had been receiving poor relief. However, it seems she was not sufficiently grateful when the Guardians offered her a position in the nurses' home at a salary of about £15 a year (less than 6s a week). She had said that as an alien's wife it was hard to find employment, so the Guardians were surprised when she declined their offer. Their initial sympathies melted away and they

Anti-German feeling on the home front: an advert for British mineral water from a Stafford firm promoting patriotic purchasing, *Staffordshire Advertiser*, 18 September 1915.

wanted nothing further to do with her case. However, one Guardian said that it was their duty to relieve those that had no resources and Mrs Schiffer had none. But his view did not prevail.[11]

Managing without the principal breadwinner was a challenge increasingly shared by many wives on the home front. In time there was a system of separation allowances for those who were dependants of men in the forces, yet there was nothing for the families of interned enemy aliens. They had to find the means to survive from within their own resources or those of their family. As a result a number were forced to seek charitable help or turn to the poor law. Moreover, the wives of interned men also had to deal with their own and their children's daily survival in the context of everyday prejudice and suspicion, as Mrs Schiffer found. Their lives were also circumscribed by increasing surveillance from the police as they fell within the system of alien registration whether or not they were German themselves, as Mrs Kuss discovered. The restrictions that followed from having to register as an enemy alien could circumscribe daily life as they included refraining from entering restricted areas (principally the east and some of the south coast – all some distance from Staffordshire), observing local curfews, and not owning various possible aids to the enemy such as cars, motorcycles, cameras and homing pigeons. Any offences under the Aliens Registration Act were punishable with significant fines or prison. This must have put even more stress on these families.

Turning to another of the German Tamworth interned 'enemy aliens', Bernard Kemper, we can see a little more of how the home front was experienced when one became an outsider. The Kemper family were living in Kettlebrook, Tamworth, in 1911. Both Bernard and his wife Emilia came from Germany but their four children had all been born in Deptford. Bernard worked with his two sons in his own sausage skin-making business. Neither his wife nor his twenty-year-old daughter had paid work, while the youngest daughter was only eleven. Bernard was a British subject, but not naturalised. By the time he was interned, he was forty-nine years old and within the target group of seventeen-to-fifty-five-year-old men who were to be detained. By November 1915 he was one of 32,440 civilian internees. His sons were twenty-one and eighteen and seem to have anglicised their forenames: Otto was now George and Paul was known as Bert. Both men were conscripted and appear in the case files of the Mid-Staffordshire Appeals Tribunal. Their position as the sons of an interned enemy alien complicated their cases. George's case was heard in May 1916. He argued to Tamworth Rural Tribunal that he should be exempted 'Because my Father is interned as a Persons of Alien enemy abstraction and I consider it inhumane to be forced to take up arms or to assist those in arms against my Father.' This was a relatively unusual position to be in, and the tribunal agreed he could have two months to get his affairs in order. However, the military representative challenged this, arguing, 'In the National interests I consider that this man should be interned or placed in a Labour Battalion.' The appeals tribunal agreed and George Kemper's temporary exemption was removed. He had to go immediately into the Army.[12]

His younger brother's case was heard immediately after George's. He made exactly the same argument and the military representative used the same words to object to the one-month exemption granted to him to wind up his business. In his case the appeal was dismissed. He then had to seek and was granted a series of short exemptions. By February 1918 his case was that his business was the only one of its kind, manufacturing sausage casings, within 30 miles of Tamworth. He was the business's manager as his brother was now in the Army and he was the sole support of his mother. The national service representative appealed against this decision in May 1918. The appeals tribunal decided in June 1918 that they had 'No Jurisdiction' over the case. This was not because of his German parents but because of his age. A royal proclamation of April 1918 had ruled that exemption certificates should be withdrawn for men born between 1895 and 1899, which included Bert Kemper.

What happened next is not clear, but it seems likely that unlike his brother, Bert remained in Staffordshire.[13]

So how did this affect the Kemper family's experience of the home front? The family remained in Fazeley. In January 1916 they took an important decision that affected the whole family's well-being: the brothers published a notice that they had taken over their father's company. It was now 'an entirely British' business and, instead of Kemper & Sons, would be known as Kemper Brothers.[18] The family do not seem to have suffered as a consequence of Bernard's internment as an enemy alien. After the war he returned to Tamworth and to the family business, which remained in his sons' names. He seems to have been fortunate. By October 1919, 84 per cent of those alien enemies who remained interned at the Armistice had been repatriated to Germany, often against their wishes. Many families were split as wives and children chose to remain in Britain. Bernard was joined by his son George, who also returned to the town after his service in the Army. During the peace Kemper Brothers continued to prosper manufacturing sausage skins. Bernard does not seem to have worried about his status as an alien, as he did not apply for naturalisation until 1931.[14]

These anxieties were not peculiar to Tamworth. At the same time as the *Lusitania* disturbances, adverts began to appear promoting a big public meeting in Hanley on 'The German Spy Peril'. The presence of Col Blizzard in the chair gave the event almost official status. Rumours from many corners of the country were re-presented to a Staffordshire audience by the well-known author of the popular anti-German invasion fantasy *The Invasion of 1910* (1906), William Le Queux. Despite the absence of local examples, Le Queux's message was plain and it did not take much for the audience to see the possible ramifications for their own county. He warned against naturalised citizens who, he said, came in all sorts of guises: hairdressers, waiters, little clockmakers and big clockmakers. He himself had found spies everywhere when he was in East Anglia. If a house was empty next to a post office in any village, they were certain to have a German trying for it. Le Queux argued the only way to deal with the German spy peril was to intern all Germans, naturalised and unnaturalised. He warned of the damage that 20,000 enemy aliens in London would do, by fomenting strikes, setting fires or guiding Zeppelins with motorcar lights.[15]

Particular events revived local anxieties about enemy aliens. The first Staffordshire Zeppelin attack led to calls for the internment of all persons of 'alien enemy birth, whether naturalised or not'. The idea was to widen the group of those interned beyond men of military age. In support of this demand, Stafford's mayor claimed that in his town there were 'still at large' ten men, eleven women and nineteen children of alien birth naturalised or unnaturalised. They could not be trusted 'and things were transpiring about them everyday'.[16]

In the summer of 1918 anti-alien feeling intensified. Stafford Council was asked to hold a meeting to demand the immediate internment of all naturalised and unnaturalised aliens of enemy blood. The council discussed how to respond. One alderman said that 'there was a general feeling that we had been too lenient with enemy aliens in this country, some of whom had been nothing more nor less than spies'. In contrast, another councillor argued there were Germans in Stafford today whose sons were fighting for this country; were they going to intern all those men who were as loyal to the king and country as anyone? Others made a distinction between the true enemy alien and the loyal naturalised citizen who happened to be of German origin. Hundreds and thousands of naturalised Germans had rendered a good service to the country and, as importantly, to the taxpayers of Britain. If these men were interned then they would have to be kept by the state. Some felt that the proposal should be limited to prohibiting naturalised or unnaturalised Germans from occupying official positions. After venting their fears and prejudices, the council decided to do nothing.[17]

Over that summer similar views were expressed in other parts of Staffordshire. This must have been unsettling to many getting on with their lives on the Staffordshire home front.

The late Lord Salisbury said:—" No living Englishman knows more of the under-currents of Europe than Mr. William Le Queux.

Victoria Hall, Town Hall, Hanley,
Tuesday Evening, May 25th, 1915, at 8 o'clock.

A Non-Political LECTURE:

"The German Spy Peril"
BY

WILLIAM LE QUEUX

the well-known writer, who for years, has made a careful study of the German Secret Service. His recent Books, "German Spies in England" and "Britain's Deadly Peril," have created a profound sensation, and certain of his suggestions have been adopted.

The Lecture is a Startling Exposure of Astonishing Facts and Outspoken Revelations.

Photo by Russell & Sons, Baker Street, W

Colonel BLIZZARD will preside.

Centre Balcony (reserved), 4s. ; Side Balcony (reserved), 3s. ; Arena, 2s. ; Gallery, 1s.
Early Doors at 7.15 p.m. FREE for all Ticket-Holders only. Commence at 8 p.m. Carriages at 9.30 p.m.
Ordinary Doors open at 7.30 p.m. for sale of Tickets on evening of Lecture.
Plan of Hall and Tickets now ready of Messrs. Webberley, Ltd., Stationers, Cheapside, and Tontine Sq., Hanley (Tel. 1178 Central).
Orders by Post receive prompt attention. Early booking suggested. Special arrangements for Schools.

A flyer for Le Queux's 'non-political' lecture on The German Spy Peril in Hanley on 25 May 1915.

Walsall Trades Council passed a resolution that all alien enemies should be interned immediately and deported at the conclusion of the war. Some recognised that there were aliens who had sons fighting in the British Army: 'While men are fighting for us, should we intern their fathers?' Others were uncompromising: one said he would shoot all Germans and argue with them afterwards, while another said that the Germans who pretended friendliness towards us might be the most dangerous. In a similar move Lichfield Council agreed unanimously in October 1918 that no person of enemy birth, whether naturalised or unnaturalised, should have any right to vote in parliamentary or municipal elections and should be prevented from becoming MPs or holders of public office.[18]

There remained uncertainty about how those known to be of German descent or who had foreign names would be treated in communities in which in many cases they were long-standing members. Although only male aliens – principally Germans and Austrians – of military age were interned, their removal could have a devastating effect on the well-being of their wives and families. They were treated as enemy aliens, whatever their country of birth, and were in some cases deported to a country they did not know. If there were such cases in Staffordshire, they have not yet surfaced. The experience of the 'enemy aliens' of Tamworth and their families seems to have been more typical of the Staffordshire home front.

Friendly Foreigners on the Home Front: Belgian Refugees and New Zealand Soldiers

The war brought people to Staffordshire who were new not only to the county but to the country. They could be termed acceptable or even friendly foreigners. The two largest groups were the Belgian refugees and the New Zealand troops stationed on Cannock Chase. What does their presence and the responses to them tell us about the Staffordshire home front?

Refugees from Belgium were a reminder to local people of what this new kind of warfare could mean for civilians. Although the number of the refugees and the pace of their arrival varied across the county, most communities offered a refuge to some Belgians during the war. By the end of September 1914 the county had received 6,000 refugees.[19] It was in response to this crisis that, as we have seen, a range of voluntary action was taken in the county to house and maintain the refugees over a much longer period than initially envisaged. This was one of the ways in which Staffordshire people 'did their bit' on the home front. But who were these newcomers and what effect did they have on the home front they joined?

The arrival of the refugees in a town often attracted a positive response. In Wolverhampton when twenty-five refugees arrived in October 1914, they received an enthusiastic welcome from crowds. The same month when a group of male refugees arrived in Hednesford, they marched from the railway station to the Drill Hall through streets lined by several thousands of people. There they met refugees who had recently arrived at neighbouring Cannock. Together they were entertained with patriotic songs of both nations and teas for all.[20]

As the county settled down to being a home front, it became clear that one way to deal with the continuing expense of this hospitality, when there were competing demands for people's generosity and the growing challenge of an increasing cost of living, was to encourage refugees to become economically independent. However, there were fears about unfair competition in the labour market. In Tamworth, the matter was raised at a fundraising smoking concert held at Kingsbury Colliery Social Club, attended by 150 people including refugees. Father Yeo, a leading figure on the Tamworth committee, explained to the audience that when the refugees first came, the committee had asked him not to find employment for the men for fear of interfering with the work of British workmen. As trade was now so good, and things in connection with the war had improved (it was now November 1914), the idea was to look for employment for the men at Tamworth. Yeo intended to keep back from their wages enough money so that when the refugees returned to their own country they would have some cash to take with them. The men were said to be anxious to work.[21]

While some workers feared competition in the labour market others tried to use the Belgians as part of their own wage bargaining. One of the branches of the Workers' Union in Burton argued in January 1915 that 30s was the least sum which an able-bodied man should receive for a fifty-four-hour week. In relation to their current wage rates, 'It was pointed out that the Belgians who are receiving the town's hospitality, to a considerable extent out of money collected from labourers, are not expected to manage on less than 25s and house, and that, therefore 23s [their current wage] was far from enough to enable a man to keep a family.'[22]

Tensions continued. At Walsall Trades Council in March 1916 complaints were made about the employment of Belgian musicians in preference to British ones, as part of a wider protest against the employment of any kind of foreign labour. One member told of a man in the town who had worked for a firm for thirty-three years, never absent or late, yet as soon as the Belgians came he was dismissed. These anxieties were not just experienced by native workers. Alphonso Slegers, aged forty-seven, had fled Belgium with his wife and three children and had been accommodated in Tunstall Park Pavilion. He got a job as a locomotive fitter at Fuller's Engineering Works. However, he worried because the factory was short of work and he thought that as a refugee he would be the first to be dismissed. He had spoken of trying to find work at Chatterley-Whitfield colliery. However, his badly mutilated body was found lying across the colliery railway line. There was discussion of whether this was suicide, but in the end the coroner's verdict was accidental death.[23]

There was also evidence that some of the refugees, although immensely grateful for the hospitality they had been given, were conscious that they were outsiders. The authorities also continued to view the refugees as foreigners who could not be expected to always understand English ways. Two Belgian refugees, staying in Wolstanton, gave an interview to the *Staffordshire Advertiser* not only to thank local people's generous response but also to give a sense of the key cultural differences they had noted, which might be affecting how they and their compatriots were responding to their new lives in the county. They contrasted the Belgian Sunday, when theatres and hotels were open to the early hours and dances were quite the thing with what they had found in Staffordshire. They said they admired the English custom of spending the day quietly at home and thought that from the evidence of their part of Staffordshire, the English were more religious. In Belgium 'ladies go to church more to show off their clothes than anything else'. They themselves were already adapting to the local culture, recognising that tea, which they were not used to, was the national drink. They thought the Englishwoman a splendid housewife and that the girls in the Potteries were tidy, did not flirt much but started work at a very young age. However, they thought beer, tobacco and tram fares were expensive. They felt the stereotype of the Englishman as phlegmatic was inaccurate. Instead,

The Englishman ... is always calm and collected. But he is very familiar with his friends, and his love of family life is something to admire. Our informants were surprised to find that the Englishman uncomplainingly gets up first in the morning, brushes his own shoes, and is not averse to facilitating the domestic work of his wife. In Belgium ... a man does none of these things.[24]

Readers of the paper might have wondered if they had met the same Englishmen as these two young Belgians.

So what do we know about the refugees who came to Staffordshire? They were a relatively diverse group who had the means and opportunity to escape to the Belgian coast, cross the Channel and then navigate the refugee relief system once they got to England. The seven refugees housed at Tutbury in October 1914 consisted of four women and two little girls but also a man who had become separated from his wife and children. The Tutbury refugees were not a single family group. What they shared was that the husbands of the women and the father of the girls were all serving in the Belgian Army. Just before Christmas 1914, the man in the group had almost given up hope of being reunited with his family and decided to take a great risk. Mr Roels, a traveller in the salt trade who had been away from his Belgian home during the German bombardment, took a tortuous route back to Belgium. He found to his joy that his family were still alive. Together, disguised as peasants, they took an adventurous journey through the war zone and managed to return not only to Britain but to the relative security of Tutbury.[25]

M. ANTOINE VAN DE BULCKE.

Antoine van de Bulcke, one of the refugees who provided a Belgian view of North Staffordshire, *Staffordshire Advertiser*, 13 March 1915.

One way the refugees were helped to manage with the strangeness of Staffordshire was to learn the language. A successful English class started in Newcastle while the movement of Belgian refugee children in and out of local schools began to be noted. For example, in Kinver in March 1915 two Belgian refugees left the district to be replaced the following month with another Belgian boy. It was also reported that Staffordshire Education Committee had

M. ARILLE HAMACKER.

Arille Hamacker, one of the refugees who provided a Belgian view of North Staffordshire, *Staffordshire Advertiser*, 13 March 1915.

decided, subject to the approval of HM Inspectot, to admit a limited number of children of Belgian refugees to Leek High School without fees. The children were often the first to pick up the language. However, as the broken English of a number of the adult refugees was often noted, local people were advised on how to communicate in the meantime. The *Walsall*

Advertiser provided a long list of vocabulary under the heading 'How to speak to the Refugees'. When a newspaper headline 'A Belgian Refugee in Trouble' drew attention to a case at Stone police court, it became clear that language was still an issue for some as the accused had needed an interpreter. The court noted that as the defendant was Belgian and had not been in trouble before, he should be discharged. However, not all Belgians found that their behaviour was excused by lack of familiarity with the local language or customs. In April 1915, Isadore Mottie, a Belgian refugee lodging in Cannock, was charged with being drunk and disorderly and assaulting a police sergeant. Although the secretary of the local Belgian Refugee Committee spoke on his behalf, Mottie was sentenced to twenty-one days imprisonment.[26]

Although Belgian refugees may have been acceptable foreigners, they were still 'aliens' and needed permission to relocate. In July 1916, Leo Jean Ledue of Stafford was summoned under the Aliens Restriction Order. He was charged that as a Belgian refugee he had failed to report his arrival in the district. It then became clear that he was not in fact a refugee, having been in England for thirty-two years. However, he had only been in Stafford for three weeks. He had previously been a hairdresser but was now working in munitions. The charge was changed to failing to register as an alien, for which he was fined £2.[27]

Belgian refugees remained on the Staffordshire home front for differing amounts of time. Alexander Maes was an eight-year-old refugee from Belgium welcomed by Knutton Committee for Aid for Refugees. The Maes family were given sanctuary at a former inn, The Old Plough, and remained there from December 1914 to October 1916. Alexander went to Knutton School while his father was given a job as a railway clerk at Stoke-on-Trent station, a similar occupation to the one he had had in Belgium. Years later Alexander still remembered members of the committee, local shopkeepers and his school teachers as well as other Knutton families. In October 1916 the family left for France. Alexander recalled years later, 'in our hearts the remembrance of the happy hours which we, poor refugees, spent at Knutton, thanks to the kindness of its inhabitants, will always remain'.[28]

Some refugee committees had less to do as the war wore on. The Walsall committee reported in December 1916 that since their formation 137 refugees had come under their care, but that most of them had obtained self-supporting employment. The Cannock refugee fund was wound up in January 1918. It was noted that £367 7s 1d had been obtained by refugees who worked in the local mines who had handed over to the fund half of their earnings. As late as 1919 two of the remaining Belgian families in Tamworth returned to their native country, leaving just two refugee families in the town.[29]

Another group of friendly foreigners who became part of the Staffordshire home front were New Zealand troops. Their presence raised rather different issues to those prompted by the arrival of Belgian refugees who were largely older people, women and children. This new group drew attention to a different matter that also had ramifications for the wider home front: the relationships between these young men and local women. The New Zealand Rifle Brigade (NZRB) was stationed on Cannock Chase from September 1917. Unlike the Belgian refugees who had few pre-existing connections with the area or even the country, New Zealanders often had strong links with Britain. They were less problematic than other foreigners for the cohesion of the home front: they made particular efforts to join in morale-boosting social events and contributed to the local economy in pubs, cafés and picture houses. Importantly, they were not competitors in the labour market or for other scarce resources nor were there problems in terms of language or culture. Unsurprisingly, the New Zealanders were seen positively and remembered fondly at a civic and personal level. Their presence in Staffordshire reveals another aspect of daily life on the home front.

Farewell parade of the NZRB, Stafford, 10 May 1919. The banner reads, 'Goodbye Dinks. Kia Ora. We'll Not Forget You'.

When the NZRB came to leave Staffordshire in May 1919, a civic farewell was organised in Stafford. This was a popular event where the cost of a gift to the NZRB of silk flags was raised by a ready response from townspeople:

It was felt they could not be allowed to go back to the Dominion without receiving some tangible expression of the good will and best wishes of the inhabitants of the county town, with many of whom they have formed lifelong friendships, cemented in not a few instances by the sacred tie of marriage.

This was not just the usual heartfelt thanks to overseas troops who had come to aid their own brave lads, although that was certainly said. The mayor's speech noted deeper bonds:

As far as the people of Stafford are concerned, I am told that some of you are already, and, judging from appearances, others are going to be not only our friends but our relatives, bound to us by the sacred bond of marriage.[30]

Certainly all the speakers, local and New Zealanders, spoke with warmth of mutual friendship but the mayor seemed to be highlighting something more.

There were a striking number of wartime weddings between Staffordshire women and soldiers from New Zealand noted in both the Staffordshire and New Zealand press. The daughter of the senior partner at the Leek solicitors, Challinor & Shaw, who were busy helping men to prepare their cases for the local Military Service Tribunals, married Lieutenant Harold Digby-Smith of the Otago Regiment in February 1918. The best man was a captain in the NZRB. Although, 'owing to the war', no invitations had been sent out, there was a large congregation at the Old Parish Church in Leek. In a New Zealand paper a touching story was told of a romantic war wedding that had taken place at Rowley Regis, Staffordshire. Driver Jack Thompson, of the Royal Field Artillery, had picked up a woman's photograph on the battlefield in France eighteen months earlier. He wrote to Maud Keightley of Rowley, whose name was on the back of the photograph, asking her if she desired its return. Correspondence ensued and the pair became engaged. They agreed to marry without meeting. Only then did Thompson come to Staffordshire to claim his bride. Local brides of other New Zealand soldiers included Elizabeth Holmes, a vocalist at Brocton camp concerts, and May Buxton, a nurse who married Sergeant William McIntosh (NZRB), a resident of St Dunstan's Institution for the Blind who as part of his rehabilitation was training to be a masseur.[31]

All these women were part of a significant number of war brides, a phenomenon that in some circumstances could worry the authorities. In 1919 it was reported in New Zealand that 2,500 of their soldiers had married English wives, 700 of whom were already in New Zealand or en route. Although there had been a good deal of criticism of 'the type of girl' the men were marrying, it was thought 'the number of unfortunate matches is very small'. New Zealand soldiers were warned, 'To Those About to Marry – Don't'. Under the heading 'Discouraging the Hasty', the detail of many hurdles a soldier had to clear to get permission to marry a local girl were outlined. These included acquiring a certificate of the bride's respectability to be obtained from a clergyman, magistrate or leading local resident.[32]

One of the reasons for this anxiety about war brides can be found in a curious report that also appeared in the New Zealand press in 1919 about a letter that had been received by the commander of the NZRB at Brocton camp.

Dear Sir – I wish to know, now that the war is over, if you have any men who want to take back wives. If so, there are three of us, and another at Brocton Camp, a WAAC, but she has got friends with one of your boys. If you have, please let me know, or put up a notice for me.

Now, I have been married. I have one daughter nearly 20, a son 9; I am 42. My daughter is the WAAC at Brocton Camp. ... The other two girls are 24 and 17. This one is a WAAC at Scotland. The one 24 is with me. Both have no home, only mine, having no mother, so now that I have lost my husband we all want to go out together. Of course, I know we cannot sail for 9 to 12 months. If you go to see my daughter she will show you my photo. I will send the other two young ladies. I will have to sell my home up. If two men would like to take us they could come here on leave, but I could not keep them in food.

I want a widower, pretty well off, one with a child or two, but best of all with none. A widower would do for Gracie, 24. Now I think I have explained all I can. If you have a lot wanting wives I will be an agent, for I am well known so I will draw to a close, hoping for the best of luck.

I remain yours faithfully, Mrs Violet - .[33]

Whether Violet's enterprising scheme was successful or whether she formally acted as a matrimonial agent is not known. However, her offer and some of the concerns about war brides linked to another phenomenon exacerbated by the presence of the NZRB on the Chase.

At the same time as the local talk of weddings, there is also evidence that the arrival of the NZRB also led to a revival of something that looked like 'khaki fever'. A number of young women came before the courts in Stafford on various charges that suggested that they were probably acting as what was termed 'amateur prostitutes', although this language was not used in their cases. 'Girls in Trouble' was the headline to a report of the case against Nancy Murrell (twenty-one) of Gloucester and Dorothy Ryan (eighteen) of Cardiff charged with sleeping out at a Midland camp. A sergeant in the New Zealand Military Police had found the girls in a building within the NZRB camp with two soldiers. Blankets were laid out and preparation made for sleeping. The girls were arrested and handed over to the civil police. This sounds like a sexual encounter. The girls had been seen in the neighbourhood of the camp for four or five weeks, and the sergeant had previously cautioned them. One girl said that her father was a soldier and both admitted that they had been in detention for a month at Birmingham as absentees from the WAAC. The girls were sent to prison for seven days. During a similar case the following week against two girls charged with entering a Midland military camp for the purpose of loitering, it was said they had been sleeping out 'practically like rabbits' – a curious turn of phrase. One girl was already on probation and both were fined £5 with the alternative of one month's imprisonment.[34]

This kind of nuisance, as this is how it was seen, had in some areas resulted in the appointment of women police. In these cases, it was one of the New Zealand soldiers who apprehended the young women and there was no mention of the deployment of women police at Brocton. However, in nearby Walsall the Watch Committee had decided to appoint two women police officers who started work in January 1918. The concern was, as the mayor said, that 'war conditions had brought women and girls into the streets more than hitherto … women police would be useful for giving help, guidance and supervision'. The latter was what was really considered crucial in relation to the moral danger that these young women were thought to pose. In May 1916 Wolverhampton had formed an Association for Outdoor Preventative and Rescue Work – essentially working with women who were engaged in prostitution or were considered to be in danger of 'falling'. Nearly two years later the chief constable spoke of the splendid job that women police were doing in the town. However, women police remained contentious. In 1919 Stoke's Chief Constable resisted this innovation: 'We do not want women on the pay of the police force and engaged in work more in keeping with Church and rescue organisations.'[35]

Rescue work had been linked to the creation of military camps in Staffordshire from the outbreak of war. In October 1914 the *Staffordshire Advertiser* published a letter that warned:

There is a universal consensus of experience that the formation of large military camps in various parts of our country has unfortunately led to most unsatisfactory behaviour on the part of a considerable number of women and girls.

Many of these are under the influence of the abnormal excitement of the times. They have not necessarily bad intentions, but undoubtedly they are running grave moral risks through exposing themselves to danger from associating with women of a much lower moral standard. They are also too

A group of NZRB soldiers in the snow at Brocton camp. They were nicknamed 'The Dinks' as they were considered to be good, honest (dinkum) soldiers.

likely to create a great deal of annoyance to the men who have so enthusiastically risen to the call of the defence of their country's honour.[36]

The arrival of the New Zealanders at Brocton camp seems to have introduced a new glamour to those in khaki. Whatever measures had already been taken, girls were still 'excited' and soldiers were still willing to spend time with them. The possible consequences of these interactions were apparent in the report of their work given by the Potteries Rescue Shelter in 1918. They noted fifty-eight girls (their term) had been through the shelter that year and that their greatest concern was the increasing prevalence of venereal disease among them. They urged that better provision should be made for treatment under suitable conditions, by which they meant something other than the traditional solution of lock wards at Stoke workhouse. The worry was that this kind of treatment would bring younger girls and the so-called 'amateurs' into touch with people of a 'depraved character'.[37] The war only worsened what was already regarded as a social problem but the concentration of many men, isolated from their families, in military camps was thought to exacerbate it. It is striking that of the three military hospitals in wartime Staffordshire, two made special provision for the treatment of VD. This was not a problem peculiar to the New Zealanders, but their presence showed that there were many ways of being friendly with the troops and different consequences for the young women as well as the soldiers.

In this context, this extract from an apparently charming poem by 'Lieutenant Dinkum', written into a local woman's autograph book by a departing member of the NZRB (known locally as The Dinks or Diggers), might read a little less light-heartedly:

> Round Brocton way it's pretty well known,
> That the 'diggers' don't stroll on the moors alone,
> So tired of themselves have the boys all grown,
> That they seek other company besides their own,
> And ere have I finished, I think I'll have shown,
> Why the 'diggers' don't walk on the moors alone.
>
> For away on the moors they go each night,
> Little brown ladies, so merry and bright,
> And the 'diggers' fall victims and well they might,
> For who could resist such a wonderful sight,
> As the WAACs on the moors in the evening light.
>
> So each 'digger' takes his lady fair,
> And they stroll off, for they know just where,
> There's a nice little possie that two can share,
> And there's no one to worry, and no one to care,
> What they say or do on the moors out there.[38]

The presence of Belgians and New Zealanders in wartime Staffordshire exposed tensions between occupants of the home front and capacities for mutual support. The next group of outsiders were not foreigners but for some they were 'the enemy'.

CHAPTER SEVEN

DIFFERENT EXPERIENCES ON THE LOCAL HOME FRONT: TROUBLESOME LOCALS OR 'THE ENEMY WITHIN'

There were a number of groups on the Staffordshire home front who were regarded for different reasons as troublesome locals such as tramps, gypsies and conscientious objectors. Some were already seen as outsiders before 1914 while others became so because of the war. They were part of the local home front, albeit in a marginal or dislocated way, and their experiences tell us more about the diverse and changing experiences of wartime Staffordshire. Moreover, the attitudes taken to these outsiders show the degree to which those in authority sought to enforce a particular version of what a loyal citizen looked like. This particularly applies to a group created by the war: the conscientious objectors.

Although pacifism as a set of beliefs existed before the war and many who would take on the label of conscientious objector (CO) were already opposed to war before August 1914, the category of CO was an invention of the First World War. Once conscription was introduced in 1916, a unique aspect of the British system of tribunals set up to adjudicate on cases for temporary or absolute exemption from military service was the inclusion of a category of exemption based upon a 'conscientious objection to the undertaking of combatant service'. No other belligerent in the First World War recognised conscientious objection to war in this way.

There are fascinating stories to be discovered about local COs. The focus here will be what their experience tells us about this particular local home front. In Staffordshire, as elsewhere, the men who appealed against conscription on these grounds were a small fraction of those who sought exemption. The cases made by COs fell broadly into two categories, which sometimes overlapped: those who had religious objections and those who objected as socialists and internationalists. Local tribunals in the county varied as to how they treated such cases. They tended to be more sympathetic to the former rather than the latter, and became increasingly wary of men who they felt had been coached by pacifist organisations like the No Conscription Fellowship (NCF) or who they thought were 'slackers' or cowards claiming to be a CO in order to dodge their patriotic duty.

A number of the Staffordshire COs were Christadelphians – a group of Christians originally formed in America during the civil war who were absolutely opposed to military service. As this sect was not particularly well known the men concerned had to explain their beliefs in order to confirm that theirs were genuine and long-held convictions. When Herbert Sykes, a twenty-one-year-old capstan lathe hand engaged in machining hand grenades at Mills munitions factory in Birmingham, submitted his case to the Lichfield Tribunal, he included

EVIDENCE

(extending over half-a-century) that

The Conscientious Objection

TO

Military Service

AND THE

Bearing of Arms

IS A

Denominational. Characteristic

OF THE

CHRISTADELPHIAN

Body of Believers

(and also of what has been done in reference to

petitioning Parliament) is set forth herein.

The pamphlet presenting the Christadelphian case against combatant and non-combatant military service used by Christadelphian COs, Appeals Case 33.

an explanation of the Christadelphian sect, a certificate of his membership, and a pamphlet explaining the Christadelphian objections to military service. Despite this evidence, it was the fact that the members of the tribunal knew Sykes and his family that persuaded them to exempt him on the grounds of his religious faith and thus his conscientious objection to combatant service. However, they would not exempt him from non-combatant service. Sykes was then forced to appeal as, he said, 'no matter what the consequences may be my faith will cause me to resolutely decline all military service, whether combatant or non-combatant'. At the Mid-Staffordshire Appeals Tribunal, Sykes's non-violent stance was interrogated at length. Although several members of the tribunal objected, the military representative taunted Sykes, calling him 'a rebel'. The apparent contradiction of making grenades despite being a CO was commented on: 'You make them, but you won't throw them?' The tribunal's decision was that Herbert Sykes had to undertake non-combatant service, but he could not accept this. What happened to him next is hard to trace. However, Christadelphians were among the COs court-martialled at Whittington Barracks, Lichfield, in May 1916. This may have been his fate, too. The court-martialled men had been arrested for failing to respond to their call-up after tribunals refused to recognise their individual conscientious objections to combatant and non-combatant military service. They were charged with refusing to obey the lawful command of a superior officer to undress for medical examination. Pleading not guilty, they argued that they were civilians. When the court allowed, they tried to explain their objections to military service. One man said that 'but for the mal-administration of the [Military Service] Act by parochially minded Tribunals he and thousands of others would have received total exemption as conscientious objectors'.[1]

So did cases like this make any difference to those who espoused Christadelphianism in wartime Staffordshire? Among the local Christadelphian COs there were members of organised groups (Ecclesia) in Burton, Cannock, Lichfield and Tamworth. The Lichfield Christadelphians, among whom the Sykes family were prominent, continued to meet

Herbert Sykes's membership card of the Birmingham Christadelphian Ecclesia, Appeals Case 33.

during the war without any opposition. In October 1914 they moved their meeting from a room adjoining St James's Hall as this was now a picture palace and was not thought to be a suitable neighbour. Instead they acquired a new comfortably heated and well-lit hall, which could seat a hundred. As a consequence they thought 'local interest in Christadelphian teaching will probably take a new lease of life'. And so it seemed, for notices announcing their two meetings each Sunday appeared throughout the war, on a number of occasions with an address from Thomas Henry Sykes, Herbert's father and manager of a local grocery store. The family do not seem to have suffered any public ill-consequences from Herbert being a CO or for the family's association with Christadelphianism. When Sykes Snr was prosecuted under a Food Order for selling bacon at too high a price and not displaying a dated list of prices, for which he was fined very heavily (a total of £55 5s), there was no reference to his beliefs or those of his son. Nor was Sykes associated with any active pursuit of a pacifist position in Lichfield, which seems to have been pretty quiet in that respect. His son, Herbert, survived the war and lived into old age. He is recorded as undertaking munitions work at the same factory in Birmingham where he had been working when his appeal was heard from February 1917 to May 1918.[2] He may well have spent the whole of the war after his tribunal undertaking this work even though, as the tribunal observed, grenade-making was rather curious work for a CO.

Other local Christadelphian COs did not fare so well. Albert Collingwood was a twenty-six-year-old cooper in Burton-on-Trent who had been a Christadelphian since 1913. His objection to combatant and non-combatant service was not upheld. He was required to present himself to the military authorities on 20 April 1916. On 29 April, he was arrested for having failed to join up and appeared in court on 1 May. Collingwood admitted the charge, saying that military service was opposed to his conscientious scruples. Although he handed the magistrates a letter explaining his situation, he was still fined £2 and handed over to a military escort.[3]

Christadelphians were the largest identifiable Christian group among the CO cases heard by the Mid-Staffordshire Appeals Tribunal, one of the three appeals bodies for the county. There was also a Christian Scientist, a Swedenborgian, a member of the Plymouth Brethren, a number of International Bible Students (today known as Jehovah's Witnesses) as well as members of Christian churches and chapels such as Baptists, Congregationalists and even the Church of England. Others, without specifying a particular affiliation, set out their personal visions of Christianity, which forbade them from killing or participating in warfare in any capacity. This shows a wide range of different religious congregations on the Staffordshire home front. Mainstream churches, Christian sects and other religious groups such as spiritualists, in their different ways, provided mutual support and solace for their adherents. There was less unanimity about the war itself and the duties of a patriotic citizen. Many more churches and chapels supported the war than resisted militarism or argued for a negotiated peace.

Applications for exemption from those who had a religious objection to war were often written in small urgent handwriting squeezing in as many biblical quotes as possible, yet others baldly stated their objection without explaining their reasons. The latter was a risky strategy and rarely led to an exemption. It shows how many men did not anticipate how the tribunal would treat their application, the questions they might be asked and the evidence they would need to prove their case. Considering what was at stake, many of those who sought absolute exemption from combatant and non-combatant services were ill-prepared for what was often a brief interrogation from a group of unsympathetic men that was usually faced alone. The antipathy was all the greater if the conscientious objection was based on a socialist and internationalist opposition to a war that was seen to only be in the interests of the capitalist class. As Edwin Wheeldon from Burton argued: 'As this war in my opinion is a

INTERNATIONAL BIBLE STUDENTS' ASSOCIATION.

In connection with "The Photo-Drama of Creation,"

An ADDRESS will be given in

THE CO-OPERATIVE HALL, VINE - STREET, STAFFORD,

On THURSDAY NEXT, at 7 15 p.m., entitled

"HELL DESTROYED : ITS PRISONERS RELEASED."

By Mr. RUTHERFORD, Birmingham.

All Welcome.   No Collection.

A Stafford meeting of the International Bible Student's Association, *Staffordshire Advertiser*, 6 May 1916.

war of class against class and not nation against nation, I absolutely refuse to take the life of innocent men or to help in any way.'[4]

This group of socialists and trade unionists was also represented among the Staffordshire COs, including those heard by the Mid-Staffordshire Appeals Tribunal. These applications also varied in their degree of fluency but many were articulate and vehement. They had to be persistent as for many tribunal members a non-religious objection was by definition not the 'genuine' objection they were tasked with identifying. Their questions in the tribunals and their private comments revealed in the Appeals papers show how difficult it was for a man to get his conscientious objection acknowledged and for him then to receive fair treatment.

Views of those thought to be shirking their duty hardened as the war dragged on. In April 1918 the military representative at Lichfield Rural Tribunal doubted the masculinity of one applicant: 'A combed out miner must not remain in the mine under any consideration. There is a place for these people afraid of shedding blood (their own) and I ask for this man to be sent to the army.' Most would have concurred with comments made by the clerk to Cannock Urban Tribunal, Charles Loxton. During the case of a nurseryman the tribunal was told that the man had 'always had a conscientious objection to war', to which Loxton replied, 'So everybody has'. Military representatives were often provocative when it came to COs. A Christadelphian who was engaged on non-combative service and applied to the Stafford Borough Tribunal to change his occupation to become a shell examiner found his motives questioned. He was not really a CO: 'He declined to go and risk his skin, but he did not mind earning 34s on work to aid the war.' A similar line was taken when the case returned to the tribunal a few months later: 'the Christadelphians seemed to be in a very happy position. Their conscience forbade them taking part in the war, and yet encouraged them to make all the money they could out of it.' Eventually it was agreed that this man should be 'put to work on the land', as a cowman on a 200-acre farm near Atherstone, at a lower wage of £1 a week.[5]

Intolerance of COs was also apparent in the wider community in Staffordshire. There was local resistance to finding work for COs who had been granted exemption from combatant service but who agreed to undertake alternative work in the national interest. In April 1916, when the volume of tribunal applications had become apparent, Tamworth Council discussed whether to appoint a committee to consider how best to make use of CO labour. They could be used in local sanitary work, attendance at asylums and other public institutions. The council was asked if it was prepared to engage such men, and, if so, what vacancies it was ready to fill. In response Alderman Evans said they could not accept the services of these men. To laughter and cheers, he said COs would be more fittingly employed as inmates rather than as attendants at asylums. They ought not to take the place of the patriotic men who were doing their duty in municipal work. The presence of these unwilling men should not be forced upon them, and they would be justified in refusing to work with them. All but one member of the council concurred with this view.[6]

Many COs could not count on the support of their churches, work colleagues or families in what was seen by many as a subversive act. However, two groups who did support individual COs can be found in the Mid-Staffordshire Appeals cases. These were the Fellowship of Reconciliation (FoR) and the No Conscription Fellowship (NCF). Both were regarded by local and appeals tribunals with suspicion or even contempt. Leslie Adams was a twenty-year-old teacher from Burton who had been a member of the FoR since July 1915. He said that,

Believing that war is a denial of the fundamental doctrine of the Christian Gospel, namely the Brotherhood of Man, and inasmuch as because it suspends the working of moral force, it hinders rather than helps the coming of the Kingdom of God, for the realisation of which I felt that as a follower of Jesus Christ my energies must be directed, I cannot take up any work which involves being part of the military organisation.

He was court-martialled at Lichfield Barracks and sentenced to six months hard labour in prison. Across the war his objection was recognised as genuine and after spending time in Derby prison, he was taken to Wormwood Scrubs to appear before the Central Tribunal as the authorities pressed COs to agree to take on the Home Office Scheme of alternative work. Adams was sent to the Weston-super-Mare timber camp and later to the work camps at Warwick and then Wakefield.[7]

Of the anti-war groups, the one that was most active in pockets of Staffordshire was the NCF. The NCF drew together many who opposed war including those who had religious objections and who were moral and political opponents of militarism, particularly socialists. One of their tactics was for members to make themselves visible at tribunal hearings to offer support to COs and to speak up for them where they could. This happened in Staffordshire. At the Walsall Tribunal in March 1916, one of the COs, who was a member of the local Board of Guardians, was accompanied by the secretary of Walsall NCF. As tribunal members said they had never heard of the organisation, he was allowed to explain that the society had been formed immediately after the war started, and was composed of men of religious convictions, including Quakers, members of the Independent Labour Party (ILP) and the British Socialist Party, who joined together on moral grounds. Soon, he too was called before the tribunal.[8]

At the Brownhills Tribunal when two farmers who were members of the NCF appealed as COs, the opinion was expressed that they had joined 'this league' for no other purpose than to escape military service. One was asked if the NCF had coached him as 'you are evidently not an extremely religious man'. He replied, 'I have had papers and bits of forms.'

He was then asked if he could repeat the Ten Commandments, to which he said he could not. 'The Chairman observed that it was obviously a case of sheltering himself behind the No Conscription League [as he termed the NCF throughout], which was an abomination.' Later he said to the other brother, 'That is precisely the same answer that your brother gave. It is one you have learned. You knew you would be asked the question.' This approach persisted at the first county appeals tribunal for the south of the county when an NCF member's case prompted the statement: 'the No Conscription League was a most poisonous society, and had done a tremendous amount of harm in one way or another. It was a sort of political gang. It was essentially not religious.' The secretary of the local NCF protested, saying, 'Members had made no attempt to prevent others enlisting. They simply catered for those of its members who wished to have nothing to do with war.' The clerk said that leaflets against conscription had been distributed, while the chairman added, 'At the present time you are running a grave risk.' The *Walsall Observer* claimed the next week that,

Every right minded trade unionist in the borough will cordially approve of the actions of the Trades Council in demanding the resignation as a member of the Naval and Military Pensions Committee of one of their number who is connected with the organisation known as the No Conscription Fellowship and whose attitude on the war has called forth their condemnation. The only regret of most people, we think, will be that the Trades Council have not asked for his resignation as a member of that body also. It cannot add to the credit, dignity or influence of any organisation of patriotic citizens to admit such men to membership.[9]

Although organised opposition to the war was not obvious on the Staffordshire home front, there was increasing anxiety about providing any opportunity for the pacifism occasionally revealed in the tribunals to surface more widely. In Walsall, there was pressure in 1916 to refuse to let council buildings to opponents of the war, such as the FoR, the Union of Democratic Control (UDC), NCF or the ILP. Pressed by the local branch of the British Socialist Party, the Trades Council urged Labour representatives on Walsall Council to strongly oppose any attempt to deprive legal organisations of their rights. One member warned the local authorities that if the halls were closed to these organisations, they would go out into the open spaces and wake the town up.[10]

By 1917 – with many local COs now in prison – another group was equally determined to awaken the town: the British Workers National League (BWNL). The balance of power in Walsall between those in the labour movement who felt opponents of the war had a right to speak and those who would deny a platform to anyone even faintly tainted with pacifism shifted during the war. The local press were more than willing to report the activities of the anti-pacifist BWNL, who became increasingly vocal in the area. Sometimes they targeted individual pacifists. In November 1916 Hanley BWNL organised a public meeting to oppose what they saw as the unpatriotic pacifism of the local MP, R. L. Outhwaite, urging that he should resign from parliament: 'every moment he sits in the House of Commons he is insulting Hanley'. More often it sought to 'out' what it saw as hidden enemies. In August 1917 the League held a 'fairly well-attended' open-air meeting in Brownhills where 'Pacifists suffered a good deal of trenchant criticism'. At one of Walsall BWNL's Sunday morning meetings, it was 'regretted that there seemed to be a big pacifist element among local labour officials'. By the summer of 1918 war weariness meant that many anxieties were voiced through the demand to search out the remaining enemies within. In Stafford, Councillor Simmons said that he thought it was men of our own race and nationality of whom the country had the most to fear, as they had been doing their utmost to assist Germany throughout the war by preaching sedition. He felt that pacifists and socialists were a much greater threat than German-born naturalised citizens. Councillor Bostock concurred: 'the greatest danger we had to face was treachery

The Russian Revolution.

Celebration Meeting

WILL BE HELD IN

The TEMPERANCE HALL, HANLEY,
On FRIDAY, APRIL 20th, 1917.

DOORS OPEN AT 7 p.m.   COMMENCE AT 7 30 p.m. PROMPT.

Councillor W. H. BEECHENER will preside.

SPEAKERS:

H. W. NEVINSON

(Distinguished War Correspondent and author of "The Dawn in Russia," and "The Growth of Freedom.")

—— AND ——

R. L. OUTHWAITE,
M.P.

Come in crowds to pay honour and tribute to the memory of the men and women who suffered and died, not only for the freedom of Russia, but for the freedom of the world.

A handbill for a Hanley meeting celebrating the Russian Revolution chaired by the ILPer William Beechener and with the pacifist R. L. Outhwaite among the speakers.

on the part of our own countrymen'. Accusations resounded around the local labour movement throughout the rest of the war, affecting the selection and support for Labour candidates at the general election at the end of 1918. The Labour candidate in Walsall 'defied anyone to prove that he had advocated pacifism'. This was the wartime climate in which men tried to get their conscientious objection to war recognised by local tribunals and in which they and their families sought to continue their lives marked by their association with something that was at the very least regarded as unpatriotic and was increasingly seen as seditious.[11]

It was hard to keep local anti-war groups going in the face of such hostility, with key members disappearing into prison. The Appeals papers show that there was a resilient group of members of the NCF in the Burton area where there was a cluster of CO cases. A significant number of these COs were members of the ILP and NCF as well as being trade unionists. Their backgrounds did not fit a single stereotype: some had white-collar jobs such as teachers or shop workers, and there were also skilled workers such as an electrical engineer. However, many worked in manual trades particularly in some aspect of the town's dominant industry – brewing.

Each CO's story is different but this example allows us to see the effect of one man's stand on his family and his connections with his community. Edwin Wheeldon was a twenty-eight-year-old grocer's assistant working for the Burton Co-operative Society when he was called up. He declared,

As a Socialist believing in International Unity and Brotherhood I cannot take part in warfare which tends to impart in the human mind the spirit of hatred and revenge. It is also against my principles as a Spiritualist and also a Trade Unionist owing to the fact that some of the men now called our enemies have been some of our strongest supporters and closest friends in the International Trade Union Movement. ... All life to me (being a vegetarian) is sacred therefore I cannot take part or help in any shape or form in the destruction of life.

The sincerity of his views was attested to by a testimonial from the Co-operative Society. He was a member of the ILP and active in his community through the Stapenhill Ward Committee of the Voluntary Aid Association, which raised money to help the poor. By the time he was conscripted those who asserted that they were COs had to reply to ten questions on the form R87, which teased out the nature, extent and longevity of their objection. These answers would then be used by the tribunals to establish whether this was a 'genuine conscientious objection'. Here Wheeldon made plain that he had joined the NCF as soon as a local branch was formed. He said that the only kind of national service that he could agree to undertake was the one he was presently engaged in:

that of fighting for the liberties which the working class as a whole are gradually but surely losing. ... I am not willing to undertake any work of National Importance that is tainted with Militarism because as a conscientious objector I am entitled by the Military Service Act to absolute exemption thereby I claim the right to live my life as I did before war was declared, trying to prove of some use to the community and earning an honest living.

He was prepared to sacrifice his personal liberty or even his life rather than stain his hands with the blood of innocent men. The Burton Tribunal rejected his claim to be a CO, because they viewed his objection as political. His appeal was refused on 31 July 1916. He was then conscripted into the South Staffordshires and after failing to comply with his call-up he was arrested, taken to Earsdon, Newcastle, to be court-martialled where he was sentenced to two years hard labour in prison. This was later commuted to one year. At Wormwood Scrubs the Central Tribunal reviewed his case and found that he was a genuine CO. He agreed to accept the Home Office Scheme of alternative work to prison and was sent to the notorious work camp on Dartmoor where other Burton COs were also imprisoned.[12]

How Wheeldon's wife and two young children coped is not clear, although his membership of the NCF meant that they would have been part of a network of support. There is also tantalising evidence that Edwin's wife Mary may have been an active supporter of his stand. The secretary of the Burton-on-Trent branch of the Women's Peace Crusade (WPC) – a grassroots women's socialist movement that pressed for a negotiated peace from the summer of 1917 – was listed in *Labour Leader* (the paper of the ILP) as Mrs Wheeldon and had an almost identical address to Edwin's. With her husband imprisoned as a CO, it would have been a brave act for Mary to raise her head above the parapet as opponents of the war were now ostracised, spied upon and generally harassed. Many of the women active in the WPC were the mothers, wives or sisters of COs. Burton was the only place in Staffordshire that had a WPC branch – one of the 123 branches that had been established by the end of the war. Long after the war in 1939, Edwin and his family were still living at the same Long Street address from which he made his application to the tribunal. It therefore seems that whatever price the family paid for their opposition to the war, it did not prevent the Wheeldons remaining part of this community for the longer term.[13]

Wheeldon's experience as a CO was mirrored by that of other Burton COs. Having failed to achieve absolute exemption through the tribunals, many found themselves arrested and then court-martialled when they refused to accept military discipline. They continued to assert that as COs, they were civilians. Jack Basham faced a series of court martials for desertion and disobedience and served prison sentences with hard labour, finally being sent to Dartmoor Work Centre in December 1918. However, others were unwilling to compromise and never accepted the Home Office Scheme. They were known as absolutists, serving a series of prison sentences in civilian prisons well beyond the end of the war. By January 1919 Joseph Clarke had served more than two years despite having been released for twenty-eight days because he was so ill. Under legislation originally designed to deal with suffragette hunger-strikers and commonly known as the 'Cat & Mouse Act', a prisoner would be allowed to recuperate briefly outside prison and would then be rearrested to serve more of their sentence. It is certainly possible that a number of the Burton COs knew each other before they tangled with the Military Services Act and some were in the same prisons and work centres during the war. To add to these possible networks which were sustained by similar beliefs and shared membership of groups like the ILP and particularly the NCF, others had family support. Burton had one family where three brothers were all imprisoned COs: Charles, Frederick and Joseph Clarke. Their sister Ethel married another Burton CO, Frederick Gilbert, in 1918.[14]

So how did an unusual family like this survive in wartime Burton-on-Trent? It is hard to tell. The labour movement was relatively strong in Burton and it included organisations that produced and supported anti-militarists, such as the ILP branch, which had been founded in 1906. Not all ILPers were opposed to the war. Another well-known Staffordshire ILPer was William Beechener, who was a Hanley councillor and sat on the Stoke-on-Trent Tribunal. His strong religious faith was his reason for participating in the enforcement of the Military Services Act. But he remained as a socialist, who saw his duty in relation to the war in a rather different way to the Burton COs. The Workers' Union was particularly active in Burton. It was one of the more radical trade unions that recruited male and female workers from a wide range of trades and prided itself on its inclusivity. Vale Rawlings, one of the Burton COs, was a founder member of the branch and was a delegate to its annual conference in 1916. By 1917 there were four branches in the town and that year the union led 3,000 local brewery workers (men, women and youths) to win higher wages in the light of the increased cost of living. However, although some of the union's members were COs and others may have been sympathetic, many more were in the forces, whether voluntarily or conscripted. One of the Burton branches of the Workers' Union had 350 members in the Army.[15]

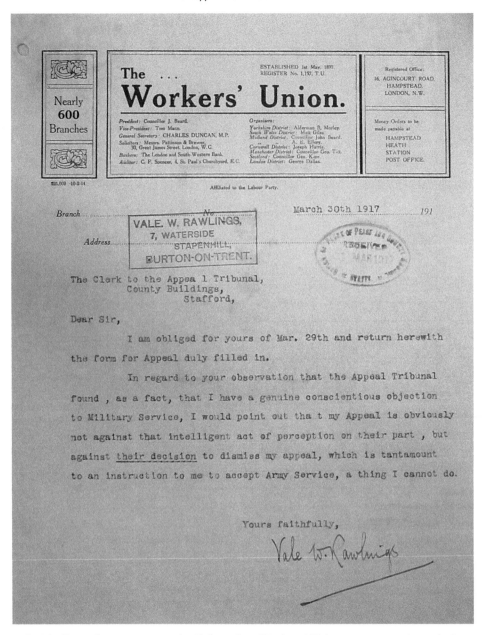

Vale Rawlings always wrote to the Tribunal on Workers' Union notepaper, Appeals Case 1334.

In terms of support for the women family members left behind by male COs, the existence of a strong Women's Cooperative Guild (WCG) in the town may have made a difference to the families of the Burton COs. In 1917 Burton WCG was holding socials that could attract nearly 300 people to dance and to play whist. Members of COs families might have been guild members, given the affiliations of their husbands or sons. Wheeldon was certainly employed by Burton Co-operative Society while another CO, Vale Rawlings, spoke at the regular quarterly meetings of the society, which in 1915 had 9,571 members. In July 1915 Rawlings argued against the society investing in war loans but failed to persuade the meeting. There were other indications of some kind of radical milieu in Burton. For example, Rawlings was listed in June 1914 as secretary of the Burton-on-Trent Daily Herald League, a magnet for progressives of all persuasions. He said he was eager to push the *Herald* to the full in Burton-on-Trent. This was a radical newspaper founded by George Lansbury that managed to keep going throughout the war by moving from daily to weekly publication, and provided some access to the kind of news that the local and mainstream press were reluctant to cover.[16]

COs knew that they would pay a personal price for their convictions. Staffordshire COs made this plain, using the wartime language of sacrifice. Edwin Wheeldon said, 'The cause for which I stand is at the present time an unpopular one therefore I have sacrificed the popularity which men in khaki are enjoying. And have also run the risk of being despised by my father and mother whose views do not coincide with mine.' Vale Rawlings, too, was very well aware of the price of being a CO:

I have long known the penalties of holding such views and have suffered for them. Neither am I forgetful of the sacrifices my wife and child will have to make as a result of my actions. Whatever may be the consequences of refusing to be militarised on this occasion, I am not prepared to sacrifice principles which I have held dear in Peace time in order to satisfy War-time hereties.

He also said that he sacrificed the prospects of a commercial career because of his socialist and anti-war opinions. The secretary of Walsall NCF said at his hearing,

If the Tribunal wished to subject him to anything worse than the calumny he had already suffered at the hands of so-called friends and Christians he was prepared to suffer the worst and had no fear of death. He admitted that he was now engaged in the manufacture of military equipment, but only did such work for the sake of his wife and children.[17]

Given the sacrifices that these men felt they were forced to make, how did their families cope with the consequences of being related to a 'conchie'? One issue was how they would support themselves particularly in provincial Staffordshire, where one might assume that they would be more isolated than in London or the larger industrial cities. Those who took on non-combatant service or work of national interest did receive a wage or allotment of sorts. However, the case was different for imprisoned COs. When the CO Leonard Lamb was charged with failing to report for military service, he was told by the Wolverhampton magistrates that the resulting fine of 40s would be deducted from his Army pay. 'Lamb said the situation appeared to him to be somewhat Gilbertian [that is ludicrously comic]. As a conscientious objector he should not perform any Army duty, and consequently he should not draw any pay.'[18] He was a member of the NCF, ILP and FoR and served a total of four prison sentences until he was released in April 1919.

Other outsiders tried to help one another, so local NCF branches raised money for a maintenance fund to help the dependants of CO prisoners who had lost their principal or only source of income. One example of a local supporter of COs and their families was Helen Wedgwood, daughter of J. C. Wedgwood MP. She was based at the family home, The Ark, near Stone, for most of the war. Like her sister Rosamund, Helen felt strongly about the CO cause. She volunteered her help to the NCF, including at their headquarters in London, sending copies of the weekly NCF newspaper *The Tribunal* up to her Staffordshire home and urging her friends to join the National Council Against Conscription. She was also active locally. In August 1917, she was still trying to recruit subscribers to the NCF. She promised a regular subscription herself when she got a new job and could see how much she could

An example of the kind of taunts faced by COs and their families, from an unidentified local newspaper, February 1916.

manage. However, she was already giving £1 a month to Stoke NCF's fund to maintain the families of imprisoned COs. She was now 'shadow secretary' for Stoke NCF covering for imprisoned members, tracking the latest arrests and court martials of COs.[19]

Although hidden from public view and certainly from reports in the local or mainstream press, there was some practical support arranged within Staffordshire for local COs and their families. Some family members may have done what the sister of the Longton solicitor, W. H. Thompson, did to support his stand as a CO. Harry, as he was known, began a series of prison sentences with hard labour after his appeal for absolute exemption was rejected at Stoke. He was arrested in July 1916 and did not emerge from prison until April 1919, having been imprisoned variously at Newcastle, Durham and Preston. As an absolutist – refusing to take part in the Home Office Scheme of alternative work – he was part of what was called the Wakefield Experiment when what were regarded as the hardcore of COs were brought together in Wakefield Prison in September 1918. It was thought they would be easier to control there and that separating them from the ordinary prison population would limit their wider influence. It was judged a failure and soon the men were dispersed back into the harsh regime of the civilian prison system.

Harry's sister, who had not shared his views of the war before his imprisonment, became an ardent supporter, following him from court martial to court martial and from prison to prison. Her son, the historian A. J. P. Taylor, who was not very sympathetic to his uncle, remembered,

Whenever he was in the guardroom, which happened for quite a long time between each court martial, she moved to an hotel in Lichfield and supplied Harry's needs for food and newspapers. Once he was in prison … She went there also. … Harry also grasped which warders were venal and put them in touch with my mother, who ran a supply of food, cigarettes and newspapers into the prison. It was almost a full time occupation. The governor left well alone, and Harry had a pretty comfortable time. [20]

Many COs had a much tougher time than this; at least seventy-three COs died because of the harsh treatment they received in prison and the work camps while a number suffered long-term physical or mental illness. Indeed, Thompson's experience may not have been as his nephew chose to remember it. Taylor was never very happy with his mother's new obsession, which included opening up her home after she moved to the Lake District to provide a place of recuperation for COs when they came out of prison. The kind of activities undertaken by Harry Thompson's sister in support of COs or the activities of Helen Wedgwood may not have been possible for those who were less well-off such as most of the Burton families. However, that does not mean that they were not able to find ways to sustain themselves despite the increasingly hostile environment.

Nor was Burton the only part of Staffordshire where what Vale Rawlings called 'outlaws' were to be found. Although Burton seems to have had a cluster of COs there were other pockets of resistance in the county. There were organised groups called Campaigns Against Conscription in Burton and North Staffordshire as well as Trades Councils in Walsall and Burton, which were identified as anti-conscription. ILP branches in Hanley and Wolverhampton were affiliated to the National Council for Civil Liberties (NCCL) and Stafford had an NCCL branch, with a woman secretary, Miss Ovenden. Wolverhampton NCF also had a woman secretary, Miss Annie Delang. [21] This is a reminder that much of the local network of support for COs and their families occurred below the radar and was reliant on the commitment of women, particularly once men of military age who resisted conscription began to be imprisoned or forced into the military.

The family of J. C. Wedgwood MP illustrate this. Rosamund Wedgwood received a letter from her father in April 1916, which expressed some concern about her support for the NCF:

About your non-conscription activities, I only want to beg you not to get into trouble with the Police while I am out of the country. Do be careful about this, because it would not be a joke to me. … Don't miss the wood for the trees; we shall have lots to do with the wood in years to come.

Nevertheless, she made enquiries about joining the Quakers and was warned by one that they were as split about the war as everyone else. Her sister Helen went to observe the treatment of COs at tribunals 'to see these fossils deciding what is to become of live people (and smashing little businesses because they are smaller than their own) maddens one'. She told her father, 'If the prospect gets too bad I shall go to prison for 6 months/1st division for distributing leaflets calculated to disturb the so-called brains of His Majesty's subjects. What a joke'. Writing from their Staffordshire home to Rosamund, their father pushed a little further on his daughters support for COs suggesting in a rather patronising way that, 'They give you quite a pleasant excitement, something to do, interesting friends and a house party for the boys.' He said that the excellent name of Wedgwood is accustomed to being made a fool of, and offered the advice 'only have at the Ark men who are gentlemen and don't talk their heads full of views they have not got; you are not to get arrested or have rows with the Potter [their uncle who ran the Wedgwood business] till I come back. Be dignified'. [23] Of course, the Wedgwood daughters were not in the same kind of danger as the Burton COs but women NCFers did get imprisoned so it is not that there was no risk.[22]

The COs, their families and supporters felt themselves to be outsiders and as the war continued they were increasingly represented as 'enemies within'. Yet they too were part of the Staffordshire home front, finding ways to survive the daily challenges of an increasing cost of living, food shortages and making ends meet just like everyone else. Although the religious and political beliefs of COs and their supporters often set them apart from their neighbours and even their families, they appear to have been extraordinarily resilient. When released, most of the Staffordshire COs returned to live with their families at the same addresses from which they had made their tribunal appeal. Moreover, many were still living there decades later. This suggests that local communities were not persuaded that these troublesome locals were actually the enemy within. Instead, they were one facet of a diverse local home front.

CHAPTER EIGHT

PEACE COMES TO STAFFORDSHIRE

The news of the signing of the Armistice reached Staffordshire on 11 November 1918. Lois Turner told her soldier brother of the response in Stone:

We got the news here about 11.30 and in less than five minutes all the bells were ringing, flags hoisted and put out of windows, fog horns going off on the railway and people dancing about. When the children came out of school fireworks were going off just like the old 5th Nov.

... All the factories were closed and the shops closed early. We all went down the town in the afternoon, all Stone was down there, there was the old band dressed in their red uniforms, and three lots of scouts playing about the town so you can tell there was some din. At night people had all their lights on, no blinds drawn down. The cinema had their big electric lights on and also Pyatts shop windows were lighted. The wounded soldiers had a big bonfire and fireworks and were allowed out till ten o'clock. And they say there was a barrel of beer in the bottom brewery yard for soldiers to help themselves to.

In Tunstall, Edith Birchall recorded the day in her diary:

Armistice Signed between England and Germany ... It was a great day for England and arrived rather unexpectedly. Things looked very black for us in March but took a complete turn this last month or so. The news landed in Tunstall at 11 o'clock when we heard the buzzers start. Soon the Market Square was thronged with men, women and children and pot girls who did no more work that day. Flags were immediately hoisted – we put 4 out. The merry-making lasted till 11 o'clock which is a very late hour for wartime – I forget it is not wartime now – I can't believe it yet.[1]

The newspapers were full of accounts of a day that had been longed for, but the tone of local reports varied. Of Burton, it was said,

the bells of St. Paul's Church were heard ringing, after a very lengthy silence, rich sounds to the ears of the townspeople. One's thoughts instinctively went back to another bell ringing in Cologne, 3½ years ago, when the Huns went mad with joy because more than 1,200 innocent men, women, and babes, had been sent to a watery grave with the *Lusitainia*, by a German torpedo. It was a glad thought today, that the power of 'the beasts' for evil had been destroyed for ever.

Others saw something rather different:

among the happy throng there were sad faces, wistful women, and unsmiling men, caused no doubt, by the recollection of dear ones lost in a great and noble cause ... above all, a great thankfulness that the war was over and that the gallant men of Britain would soon return.

In the coming days, the sense of triumph abated and many had conflicting emotions. Edith Birchall headed her first entry in 1919, 'Peace!' and made a New Year's resolution: 'To meet life courageously'. A few months later the young teacher reflected: 'I wish I could feel more peaceful & settled. I suppose lots of women are having the same experiences. NY Resol is hard to keep but the best I could have made.' Just as the war came slowly into the lives of Staffordshire people, so the demobilisation of the home front and the making of peace took time and affected people in different ways.[2]

Everyone was anxious to see their men home as soon as possible. Lois Turner wrote to her brother in December 1918:

What are you doing in Palestine now? Is there any talk of you coming home? We hear all sorts of rumours here, one is that the Staffs - Yes! - are on their way home. I only hope that it is true. What a day that would be when you come once more to dear old Stone.

The Armistice did not bring the soldiers and sailors home immediately. Like everything else on the war and home front, it had to be organised. Some soldiers had priority. Fuel shortages meant miners were particularly needed. It was estimated that the first 100,000 would be released by the end of 1918 at the rate of around 5,000 a day. Some of them were returning to Staffordshire. Farmers could also apply for men to be released early from the Army to return to work on the land as maintaining food production was as urgent as during the war. These cases took a great deal of Eustace Joy's time at the War Agricultural Executive Committee in the months after the Armistice. In March 1919 Mrs Wilding asked him if there was anything that could be done to get her husband home. He had been a POW in Germany, completed his two months leave and had now returned to his depot in Preston. She explained that he was a one-man business, farming 80 acres. She pleaded, 'If you could do me the favour of getting him home altogether or even an extension of leave for a fortnight or so in order to get the ploughing etc done. I have absolutely no one else to rely on and it will put me in an awful fix if he does not return soon.' There were regulations concerning the manpower requirements of the peace that had to be made to work by balancing the competing demands of the military, employers, ex-servicemen and the home front workforce. Joy was a central figure in this process in Staffordshire.[3]

As well as the release of the men in an orderly fashion, the home front had to organise to deal with the effects of military and civilian demobilisation. One of the issues was matching demobilised soldiers and unemployed war workers with peacetime jobs. Tamworth quickly reopened its Employment Exchange together with a second temporary one at the Baths, Church Street. Here they administered out-of-work donations to those demobilised from HM Forces and to civilian workers now unemployed because of the termination of war contracts. The rates of payment from December 1918, which were published in the local press, were 29s for adult men, 23s for adult women and lower rates for boys and girls between fifteen and eighteen years old. There were also additional payments for dependants. Civilians were to be paid for thirteen weeks while for those demobilised from the military payments would last twenty-six weeks. Employers could also apply to the Exchange for the return of men from the forces or correspond directly with former employees to get their agreement to early release. The previous manager of the Tamworth Labour Exchange had been specially demobilised so that he could resume his work.[4]

Rising unemployment unsettled everyone after the full employment of the war. When the closure of the National Machine Gun Factory in Burton was announced in May 1919, 200 out of the 250 jobs were lost. In June 1919 there were 145 discharged sailors and soldiers out of work in the immediate area of Stafford with a further forty men seeking employment. Women struggled too as local cases of unlawful claims for out-of-work payments show. Annie Peat, twenty-one, came before the Stafford bench. She had been discharged from Bagnalls engineers and claimed to be available for work. She was charged with not declaring one and a half days work as a kitchen maid prior to her claim. Although she said she did not regard this as her last employment, Annie was fined £5 or a month's imprisonment. 'A good deal of that kind of thing was going on', said the magistrate. However, what the case reveals is how difficult it was for young women discharged from better-paid war work to find employment with equivalent wages. Many were forced back into domestic service or low paid work such as a kitchen maid. This had consequences for families as well as for the labour market.[5]

It is not surprising that industrial unrest characterised the year after the Armistice. In Staffordshire as elsewhere the unions continued to press for wages to keep up with prices, so sanitary workers employed by Tamworth Council were awarded an immediate rise of 10s a week in November 1918. There were strikes in the county, including bakers and agricultural labourers, and most of all there was uncertainty. J. C. Wedgwood MP observed in February 1919 that 'unemployment is rife in the Potteries, and will become universal if and when the coal strike occurs'.[6] Managing the labour market was difficult and explains the continuity of most of the wartime controls and regulations into the post-Armistice period. What it meant for households who had struggled through four and a half years of war could be acute hardship coupled with increasing frustration.

Everyone felt they had a strong case and without the shared purpose of the war, earlier tensions were made more explicit. A couple of reader's letters to the *Burton Daily Mail* show this:

Sir – What is wrong with some of the employers of Burton? … There are, at the present moment in Burton, men who have done their bit, and some of them a big bit. They came home thinking that a grateful town would see to it that they were not short of a job. What do they find? … Women in shops, women on cars, women railway porters, women this and that … With all respect to the women who came to the rescue at a time when the men-folk answered the call, I take it that their work is done, and they ought in honour to themselves to retire and to give those who have been fortunate enough to come back a chance. BYSTANDER.

Just like the war: bread queues in Stafford during the bakers' strike, 1919.

Sir – Will you kindly allow me to answer the discharged soldier who is asking the women to kindly return to their hearths and homes? A great many have done: some are left behind to finish, like myself and my workmates who are maltsters. That is entirely left to the head employers as long as they think fit to keep us. When we get our discharge we will all return to our hearths and homes and make room for you all. The country has been glad of the women's labour while such as you were taken from home, and all have done their best on both sides, especially when it came to seven days a week. Can the discharged soldier do the malting, for it takes some doing? The women have done their best.

    Yours, a LATE SOLDIER'S WIFE AND MALSTER.[7]

Demobilisation did not always run smoothly or meet everyone's expectations. Returning soldiers and sailors had already formed their own organisations during the war and soon were active in the politics of towns across the county. In July 1919 Longton and Fenton branch of the National Federation of Discharged & Demobilised Sailors and Soldiers (NFDDSS) held a meeting protesting against employers who had refused to reinstate ex-servicemen in their jobs as had been promised during the recruitment campaign. There were NFDDSS candidates in Staffordshire's first local government elections after the war in October 1919. W. T. Richardson topped his poll in the east ward, Stafford, while the secretary of the Ex-Soldiers Federation defeated a long-standing councillor in Burton. Nor was it just the needs of demobilised men that were raised. At a Uttoxeter district committee of the Women's War Agricultural Committee in December 1918, the women wanted to see ex-servicewomen having the same kind of facilities for training for useful work as were being provided for men. They thought rural industries would be particularly appropriate.[8]

Daily Life in the Transition to Peace

The period of transition between the Armistice and the peace treaty was one of uncertainty when it came to managing everyday life. In January 1919 much was made of the government report that confirmed what Staffordshire citizens knew: the war had seen a significant increase in the cost of living. Weekly expenditure on food for a standard family had risen from 24s 11d in June 1914 to 47s 3d four years later. Nor did the Armistice stop the continuing rise in the cost of living. The *Staffordshire Advertiser's* leader on 25 January was entitled 'High Prices and Unrest'. It worried that 'unless the Government tackle the question in real earnest the country will drift into a state of chaos'. It was particularly alarmed that the high prices of the necessaries of life were forcing workers to press for higher wages. While retailers, wholesalers and producers were pushing for the removal of wartime controls, the *Advertiser* warned against this. More troubling was 'the conviction of the workers that they are being shamelessly exploited in order to satisfy the greed of the profiteer'. This had to be tackled 'with a stern disregard for any vested interests which may stand in the way of the general welfare of the community'. Yet this was not the only injustice: many of the not yet demobbed soldiers were bitter that the government had readily granted 25s unemployment pay to 'the overpaid munition worker' while a soldier's wife had a paltry 12s 6d a week to keep the home going. This was not the peace that people had dreamed of; instead the paper called for the government to act 'in a fair but resolute manner'. 'If they do not do so at once they will simply play into the hands of the extremists, who desire nothing better than to see this country in the throes of a revolution like that which has brought Russia to ruin.'[9]

    In Staffordshire homes there were still real challenges. There were significant fuel shortages. The first Christmas of the peace saw an acute shortage of coal, which it was hoped that the returning miners would soon begin to solve. In the meantime it was essential that rationing remained in place. The Coal Controller explained:

People had been buying more coal than they needed because of fear for the future, but that was not wise, and prevented others from getting their fair share. The present acute pinch – which was quite as serious as it had ever been – had arisen because influenza was affecting labour, while the short days, bad weather and fog all had a serious effect upon output and distribution.[10]

He also warned there would be no relief from rationing that winter.

Food control also continued. There was an attempt to make the first Christmas of the peace better than those in wartime. The Food Controller made various concessions because of the season: a coupon was not required for poultry and game but maximum prices applied; the sugar coupon for Christmas was increased by 4oz and there were also various coupon-free meats such as offal and tinned rabbit. Some rations increased: in January 1919 the ration grew to 1oz butter and 5oz margarine while some controls were lifted such as for tobacco. Commercial adverts made much of goods coming off the rations: 'TEA is free from control today. Now try a cup of Lipton's' appeared in March 1919. At the same time bakers were still fined for selling 'new bread' without a licence. The FCCs went about their business together with new Anti-Profiteering Committees. Policies adopted on the home front were extended into the peace: in September 1919 Hanley opened a new National Kitchen while after a lengthy discussion Stafford Council decided to leave the idea alone.[11]

For others the year after the war was a time of opportunity. The Zetland Café in Stafford was relaunched with a half-page spread in the *Advertiser*. High-class cuisine was offered with an orchestra from 3 to 7 p.m. daily, together with a bakery. It was run by a husband and wife team. Agnes Woolley had run the café alone after her husband had enlisted, advertising throughout the war for waitresses and shop assistants. George had been demobbed in March 1919 after serving for most of the war as a catering instructor to both the English and American armies. It was said, 'So popular are these toothsome delicacies that Mr Woolley finds it well-nigh impossible to keep pace with the demand'.[12]

A treat at the Zetland Café might have brightened daily life as the Staffordshire home front made the transition to peace. It was unlikely to overcome the persistent anxiety about when family members would return from the front, from imprisonment as a POW or even from a CO work camp. To add to this strain, the influenza epidemic affected the county in waves in 1918 and 1919 and meant some hardly noticed the Armistice. Many school log books do not note the end of the war because they were closed due to the epidemic. Different parts of the county were affected at varying levels of intensity but there was a high death toll, particularly among children. In Stoke there were sixty-four deaths in the weeks leading up to 26 October 1918 and in an earlier outbreak in July and August 130 had died. In the same month Burton was battling influenza, schools were closed and there was difficulty in maintaining the railway service because of illness. Sixty-six people died in the town from influenza in the week ending 1 November. By March 1919 the epidemic was thought to be in decline in the Potteries: only forty-three had died from influenza the previous week while a month before the weekly death toll was seventy-five. New Zealanders at Brocton camp were also among the victims. When the NZRB left Staffordshire, seventy-three of their comrades were buried in the camp cemetery, of which at least forty were victims of the influenza epidemic. The pressure on local hospitals was severe. In Cannock the Board of Guardians were requested to release two workhouse nurses temporarily to nurse cases of influenza. It was argued that, 'People were dying for the want of attention, and a number of trained nurses were required'.[13]

Picture House, Stafford

TO-DAY, SATURDAY—

THE WOMAN IN WHITE.

From Wilkie Collins' Novel.

MONDAY, TUESDAY, and WEDNESDAY—

20,000 LEAGUES UNDER THE SEA.

From Jules Verne's phantasy which became facts.
Suitable for Patrons of all ages.

THURSDAY, FRIDAY, and SATURDAY—

The Turn of a Card.

With the popular Favourite, WARREN VERRIGAN.

FRIDAY, DEC. 6,—

Special Matinee for Queen Mary's Needlework
Guild, under the patronage of Lady STAFFORD.

All Proceeds this week for the KING'S FUND.

Particulars in another Column.

To comply with an Order issued by the Local Government
Board, and to remain in force during the influenza epidemic,
the Hours of Performances until further notice will be :—

Evenings, one performance only, 7-30 to 9-30,

Matinees, 2-30 to 4-30

Saturday, the continuous system will be entirely discon-
tinued, and Performances will be 2-30—4-30, 6—8, 8-30—10-30.

PATHE GAZETTE AND GAUMONT GRAPHIC IN EACH
PROGRAMME.

Telephone 291.

The influenza epidemic changes the weekly programme of the Picture House, Stafford,
Staffordshire Advertiser, 30 November 1918.

Steps were taken to inhibit the spread of the epidemic. In November Cannock UDC asked proprietors of places of entertainment to clear buildings between performances so that they could be thoroughly ventilated. In Stafford the Picture House programme noted that because of influenza, the continuous Saturday showings were to be ended. There was still a sense that people were uncertain how to respond to influenza, so in February 1919 a leaflet outlining the precautions to be taken was distributed to each household in Stafford.[14] Anxieties about the epidemic changed aspects of daily life particularly the gathering of large groups of people together, including for celebrations.

Celebrating Peace

Some towns and villages in Staffordshire organised welcomes for returning soldiers and repatriated prisoners. In January 1919, 98 of the 120 Tamworth men who had been POWs were entertained to a dinner by local dignitaries and the Chamber of Trade's Soldier's Parcel Fund.[15] However, the main effort went into planning events that would only begin once the peace treaty was signed and the war was truly over. This is the reason for many war memorials dating the end of the Great War as 1919.

Meanwhile there was also a need to acknowledge the individual achievements of the war. In May 1919 there was time to properly recognise the heroism of Burton's William Coltman VC, the most decorated other-rank soldier of the war, who had just received his medal at Buckingham Palace. All the stops were pulled out for the civic reception at Burton where he was presented with a war bond of £145 and a handsome marble timepiece. Coltman was gracious, saying 'such distinctions had been earned in many cases which had not been recognised'. He was one of four men who represented the town's battalion, the 6th North Staffordshires, in the great victory march in London on Peace Day. In most of these accounts the fact that Coltman was a stretcher – bearer rather than a fighting soldier was not mentioned. It complicated the stories now being told.[16]

Not everyone was sure that celebration was what was needed. In Stafford there were divisions within the council on who should pay for the peace celebrations but also whether they were appropriate. One councillor said, 'He rejoiced that the Germans had been beaten, but he saw no reason for jigging or dancing over them, and he objected to money being spent in revelry and in drinking and feeding.' However, another councillor pointed out that at least 500 disabled soldiers would participate in Stafford's peace celebrations and their services ought to be acknowledged. Councillor Deakin said,

the country had willingly spent money on the war and killing people, and he did not see why money should not be voted to celebrate peace. He would not like to think he belonged to a town which was so mean and miserable as to have no peace rejoicings. Stafford would be a laughing-stock to the rest of the country.[17]

The peace treaty was signed on 28 June and the government decided that there would be a national Peace Day on 19 July 1919. The inhabitants of Stafford received the news of the treaty 'very quietly indeed' and there was no organised demonstration. However, that did not stop spontaneous celebrations. 'The juveniles made the most of the occasion, and organised imitation Jazz bands, parading the streets with tiny flags and beating tin cans etc. The din which was created can be more imagined than described.' In the evening soldiers from Brocton camp came into the town. They let off crackers to the alarm of women in the crowd but, 'There was no semblance of riotous behaviour … on their part, and realizing what the end of the war means to many still in khaki, the citizens sympathised with the exuberance of their military neighbours.'[18] There was also a thanksgiving service involving the six churches of the borough.

A thanksgiving service 'In Memory of Our Fallen Heroes', organised by the National Federation of Discharged and Demobilised Soldiers in Stafford, 24 August 1919.

In Burton it was said that the signing had been postponed so often that the official news of the peace took many unawares. Dozens of brewery buzzers accompanied by the discharge of maroons drew thousands of people into the streets where they formed informal processions and sang popular songs. The inhabitants of North Staffordshire 'while accepting the news with satisfaction, reserved their rejoicings for the official day of peace celebration. There was little demonstration'. A beacon that had been erected by the residents of Sneyd Green, Hanley, was prematurely set alight to the indignation of those who had gone to the trouble of building it in readiness for the official peace celebrations. In Wolverhampton the central part of the town resembled Armistice night, with ex-soldiers and men on leave engaging in impromptu dancing. There were fireworks and a concert by the choir and children of Bethel Church in West Park on Sunday night.[19]

Peace Day was celebrated in Staffordshire in much the same way as elsewhere. There were festivities throughout the county, although some of the villages decided to postpone their celebrations to a later date. The idea was that no one should be excluded: in Stafford over 500 old people were treated to breakfast and each was presented with a packet of tobacco or tea. One of the organisers of the breakfast, Mr Peach, explained the mixed emotions surrounding the peace celebrations:

There was a sad side to the celebrations and some good people thought these rejoicings were out of place, but he did not agree with them. It was right to mourn with those that mourned, and they had done so. Those who had been bereaved knew that they had their heartfelt sympathy, but it was also right to rejoice with those that rejoiced, and to be thankful for millions whose lives had been spared, and that victory had crowned their efforts ... They did not forget that their freedom and liberty had been bought with a price.

The Stafford MP, Captain Ormsby-Gore, also considered the meaning of the peace celebrations for the home front and, more unusually, included women in his reflections:

the first duty of a day like that – to pay a large tribute to their fighting men and to their women, who had shown the fighting spirit ... They still had difficulties ahead, and it was only by maintaining their war spirit that they could win through to the end and have peace in their homes.[20]

The scale of events varied. In Bradley about 300 sat down to a knife-and-fork tea laid on in the schoolroom while in Walton there was a treat for all the village's children and a tea for the widows. An entertainment for returned soldiers was planned for August as so many had not yet come home. Some celebrations focused on the war rather than the peace: in Penkridge there was a big procession with tableau followed by a presentation of medals to the gallant men of the war. In Burton, thousands of people watched the parade, which included 2,500 members of the NFDDSS, some of whom wore khaki. The other theme was fire. Stafford Council spent £50 on its firework display while Lichfield not only held a torchlight procession but lit a huge bonfire, 22 yards in circumference and 25-foot high.[21]

After Peace Day, the big decision in communities across the county was what form their memorialisation should take and who was to be remembered. In Stafford a Peace Celebrations Committee was appointed to organise the town's considered response to the end of the war. There was no unanimity about the best way to acknowledge the sacrifices of local soldiers and sailors. Discussions between the committee and ex-servicemen,

Celebration meal for returned soldiers in Market Hall, Rugeley, 1919.

mostly members of the local branch of the NFDDSS, raised the kind of concerns expressed elsewhere in the county. It was agreed that a proposal to give a dinner for the silver-badge men (soldiers discharged during the war, usually for health reasons including wounds) had been rightly refused as it was felt that all who had gone to war should be recognised. An idea that all men who resided in the borough who had served should be issued with a certificate was also rejected. More were in favour of the idea that a club should be provided for ex-servicemen: the YMCA was not felt to be an adequate substitute, as they wanted a club of their own. There was also a heated discussion on whether the NFDDSS spoke for all servicemen. It was said to only include 600 of the 4,000 men who had gone from Stafford. A suggestion was made that some of the money (the mayor said £175 had been raised) should go to the disabled but a disabled soldier said he did not want to be made more fuss of than the men who had been four and a half years in the trenches and had not been wounded. The meeting broke up in disorder before a decision was made.[22] There were not only different views of whose sacrifice should be commemorated but also what constituted a fitting memorial.

Commemoration and Memorials

Well before the war ended, there was talk of how to commemorate it. Memorial services were held throughout the war for individual men or in particular communities, but soon more lasting memorials were erected. An early one was commissioned in November 1915 for Denstone College, a boys' school near Uttoxeter. A Mother's Window to commemorate 'the sacrifices which mothers and women are so willingly making' was dedicated on All Soul's Day 1916.[23] Churches indicated what kind of gifts might form suitable memorials while Walsall Council formed a committee to plan a local war memorial in 1917. Memorial tablets to the dead were unveiled before the end of the war, such as at the Primitive Methodist Chapel in Walsall in February 1918 while in the summer of that year Hednesford was considering creating a public park as a memorial.

There were many different local funds raising money for scores of memorials, although there was less consensus on the form that memorials should take. By the time of the Armistice local councils were asking for ideas. Public meetings were held at Cannock and Hednesford where it was suggested that people wanted public baths or a public free library for the whole area or, as an alternative, a cottage hospital for Cannock and a public hall for Hednesford. The council intended to use the £4,000 it had invested in war loans to fund the war memorial. To begin with there was at least as much focus on an amenity for the living than a monument commemorating the dead. In Burton suggestions included a people's recreation hall with a winter garden, almshouses for men crippled in the war and scholarships for orphans of soldiers and sailors or a general fund for the widows and dependents of the fallen. Once memorialising entered the realm of formal committees many of the suggestions to benefit the ex-soldiers or those widowed or orphaned through the war got lost. Meetings were held to measure public feeling and as a prelude to setting up local funds. In the meetings in Stoke in early 1919 many said the first thought should be for the widows and orphans, yet eventually the much smaller fund than anticipated was used to support North Staffordshire hospitals and to erect a monument. In Rugeley it was found that the proposed recreation ground was impracticable, public baths could not be self-supporting and ordinary baths were not thought a fitting memorial. In the end it was decided to erect a statue. In contrast in Trentham a well-attended meeting wanted a fund to be raised to assist the dependents of the fallen from the village and to provide help for the wounded and the disabled. A cross would be erected to commemorate the war service of villagers – a wider group that the military war dead.[24]

This memorial window in St Luke's Church, Cannock, was dedicated in 1917. It was given by Charles Loxton, clerk to Cannock Urban Tribunal, in memory of his son Edward who was killed on the Western Front in 1915.

Memorialising soon became as much about demonstrating civic pride and competing with other local towns in their public displays as meeting the more immediate needs of surviving soldiers or the widows and orphans left by soldiers killed in action. In Wolverhampton, the scheme for a Memorial Hall was dropped in April 1919 when donations were not forthcoming at the required scale. One councillor attacked the organised discharged soldiers and sailors who were making their voice heard across the county. He felt they 'were destroying a movement for the proper recognition of the services of their comrades'. In Walsall there were rumours that some ex-servicemen were not satisfied with what had been done for them, but Mr Connor of the local branch of the NFDDSS said the discontent was created by agitators, many of whom had never been out of the country. He felt servicemen had received every consideration. The unity that had been found to sustain the home front was disappearing quickly. There were even two competing organisations speaking for Staffordshire's former soldiers: the NFDDSS, a rank and file organisation with links to the labour movement, and the more official Comrades of the Great War. The latter had 800 members in Wolverhampton and 250 in Hednesford. Lord Dartmouth observed that 'unless there was some combination between them there would always be suspicion and jealousy of each other'. Nationally, the groups would merge to form the British Legion in 1921.[25]

Once the focus turned to monuments rather than amenities as memorials, there seemed to be some competition as to size: Stoke's planned cenotaph was to be over 24 feet high while Burton's was 30 foot. As well as churches and chapels, businesses erected their own memorials. Lichfield Brewery unveiled an artistic mural in front of their offices in memory of thirteen employees killed in the war. Siemens' war memorial was unveiled on Armistice Day 1920 with eighty-nine men's names on it. It had been funded by subscription from the workforce. Wrapping in the survivors to the ceremony, the company noted the promise they had made in August 1914: dependents of those who enlisted should be provided with such assistance as would keep them in reasonable comfort; and that those who returned should be taken back into the service of the company. Every effort, they said, had been made to fulfil these promises and, as far as was known, every man who returned (520 men returned of the 834 who went) had found the promise fulfilled. There were 2,500 at the opening ceremony but it was also filmed so that it could be viewed at local picture houses.[26]

Aside from parish, town and works memorials there was also discussion of a county war memorial. This official initiative took time to get going. By November 1919 it was clear that they wanted both a visible monument commemorating the names of those who had fallen and also to try to do something from which the survivors would benefit. They did not want to interfere with local memorials but they too would be looking for subscriptions when there were many demands on local people. The William Salt Library was trying to assemble a complete list of Staffordshire men who had lost their lives in the war, but thus far there had not been a particularly good response from the parishes that had been circulated. One of the few women present, Mrs Bolton, suggested that in view of the work that women had done during the war, they should be represented on the Memorial Committee. However, there did not seem to be any question of commemorating women's service on the memorial itself.[27]

Few thought that those who had contributed to the resilience of the home front should be remembered in formal memorials. However, certain sorts of war service at home were recognised after the war by awarding honours to those who had led the voluntary effort in the county. Of the 6,000 national honours awarded for services rendered in connection with the war, some of the Staffordshire recipients were predictable such as the Countess of Dartmouth, who was awarded a CBE as president of the county Red Cross Society, or Col Wetheral of Rugeley, county director of Auxiliary Hospitals and VADs in Staffordshire. However, among the OBEs was a greater range of voluntarism and volunteers such as Mrs Loder-Symonds for providing the refreshment buffet for soldiers on Lichfield Trent Valley Station or Arthur du Pre Denning, joint secretary of Stafford War Savings Committee. Among the MBEs awarded to Staffordshire people was one for Mrs Ada Nicholls, secretary of Lichfield War Pensions Committee.[28] With a few exceptions, ordinary men, women and children of the home front were not formally remembered and were almost never referred to in the ceremonies and monuments that constituted official commemoration of the First World War. Staffordshire was no different in this respect from most of the rest of the country.

Once they were complete, the opening ceremonies of town memorials refocused attention on the grieving widows and orphans. When Lichfield's war memorial was unveiled in October 1920 the crowd was said to be

Staffordshire County War Memorial, Stafford, was unveiled in 1923.

fittingly representative of every class and section of the community, this being particularly applicable to the bereaved, who created considerable emotion amongst the huge congregation as they laid their floral tributes to their loved ones at the foot of the gold-coloured monument to the strains of … Chopin's 'Marche Funebre'.

It was noted with pride that this was the first memorial of any importance to be completed and paid for in the county. It had 209 names on it. Other memorials faced delays such as in Hednesford where the coal strike had meant that that they had not been able to raise the necessary funds to meet the cost of a memorial. In November 1920 there was some confidence locally that the situation would soon improve so a tender for a 21-foot monument had been accepted at the cost of £1,215.[29]

The opening ceremony of Eccleshall's memorial allowed for a slightly different emphasis as the first name on the list of those who died in war was Annie Elizabeth Allen VAD. Of a local population of 2,500, 350 had answered the call and forty-four had fallen. Lord Dartmouth, who spoke at the unveiling of many of Staffordshire's memorials, said on this occasion,

There was one thing that distinguished the Eccleshall Memorial from many others which he had been connected with, and that was that it included the names of women, who played such a splendid part throughout the war. When the official history of the war came to be written, one of the finest chapters would be that which described the women … Concerning the points of similarity, in these days of unrest, suspicion and jealousy it was something to find one thing, and that was they were all British and ready to do honour to the men who gave their lives … the finest and most lasting memorial they could put to those who had fallen was to do what they could for those who were living.[30]

That was the challenge more generally in winding down the home front and building a peace.

NOTES

All manuscripts are located at the Staffordshire Record Office unless otherwise indicated.

1. War Comes to Staffordshire

1. Edith Birchall diary, private collection.
2. J. C. Wedgwood to 'My dearest girl', 3 September 1914; Charles Wedgwood to Josiah Wedgwood, September 1914, JCW/7, Josiah Clement Wedgwood Papers, Special Collections and Archives, Keele University Library.
3. All quotations in this chapter come from *Staffordshire Advertiser*, 8 August 1914, unless otherwise indicated.
4. *Cannock Advertiser*, 8 August 1914.
5. *Daily Telegraph*, 26 September 1914.
6. *Wolverhampton Worker*, September 1914.

2. Creating a Home Front

1. *Staffordshire Advertiser*, 31 October 1914; *Tamworth Herald*, 7 November 1914.
2. *Tamworth Herald*, 21 November 1914.
3. *The British Clayworker*, September 1903, in Colonel Blizzard's Scrapbook, D797/2/1; *Staffordshire Advertiser*, 23 January 1915; 'Blizzard's Bold Brigade', Colonel Blizzard's Scrapbook.
4. Typescript, Colonel Blizzard's Scrapbook.
5. *Staffordshire Advertiser*, 20 March 1915; 27 February 1915.
6. *Staffordshire Advertiser*, 3 April 1915.
7. Newspaper cutting, 3 May 1915, Colonel Blizzard's Scrapbook.
8. Newspaper cuttings, 3 May 1915, 10 May 1915, Colonel Blizzard's Scrapbook:
9. *Burton Daily Mail*, 24 January 1918
10. *Birmingham Daily Post*, 10 April 1915.
11. *Staffordshire Advertiser*, 8 May 1915.
12. *Staffordshire Advertiser*, 1 May 1915; 20 November 1915.
13. *Staffordshire Advertiser*, 23 October 1915.
14. *Staffordshire Advertiser*, 4 March 1916; 18 December 1915.
15. *Lichfield Mercury*, 28 August 1914.
16. *Staffordshire Advertiser*, 10 October 1914.
17. *Staffordshire Advertiser*, 9 January 1915; 30 January 1915; 27 February 1915.
18. *Tamworth Herald*, 26 September 1914.
19. *Staffordshire Advertiser*, 20 March 1915; 17 April 1915.
20. *Staffordshire Advertiser*, 8 May 1915.

21. *Staffordshire Advertiser*, 24 October 1914; *Lichfield Mercury*, 29 January 1915; 17 September 1915
22. *Lichfield Mercury*, 5 February 1915
23. *Lichfield Mercury*, 26 March 1915.
24. *Walsall Advertiser*, 5 September 1914.
25. *Staffordshire Advertiser*, 30 January 1915.
26. *Staffordshire Advertiser*, 8 May 1915.
27. *Staffordshire Advertiser*, 18 September 1915; 22 January 1916.
28. *Staffordshire Advertiser*, 5 February 1916.
29. *Staffordshire Advertiser*, 5 February 1916.
30. *Staffordshire Advertiser*, 5 February 1916; 12 February 1916.
31. *Burton Daily Mail*, 31 July 1916; *Staffordshire Advertiser*, 12 February 1916.
32. *Staffordshire Advertiser*, 12 February 1916; 26 February 1916.
33. *Staffordshire Advertiser*, 5 February 1916; 4 March 1916; *Burton Daily Mail*, 9 October 1916; *Cannock Advertiser*, 26 February 1916.
34. *Staffordshire Advertiser*, 7 October 1916
35. *Staffordshire Advertiser*, 12 January 1918; 7 December 1918.
36. W. Martin, *A Minstrel in Staffordshire* (W. D. Bell, Stafford, 1923), pp.33,48.
37. Edith Birchall diary, 27, 28 November 1916.
38. *Staffordshire Advertiser*, 1 April 1916; Mid-Staffordshire Appeals Tribunal Case 124.
39. *Great Western Railway Magazine*, August 1916; *Staffordshire Advertiser*, 23 June 1917.

3. Making a Living on the Staffordshire Home Front

1. *Leek Times*, 1 April 1916.
2. *Staffordshire Advertiser*, 1 May 1915; 14 August 1915; 2 October 1915.
3. *Staffordshire Advertiser*, 23 October 1915; 12 February 1916; 15 April 1916.
4. *Staffordshire Advertiser*, 26 August 1916.
5. *Staffordshire Advertiser*, 23 September 1916; 4 November 1916.
6. *Staffordshire Advertiser*, 1 September 1917; 29 June 1918.
7. *Tamworth Herald*, 31 March 1917; Sarah Hay to Eustace Joy, 21 September 1918, C/C/M/4/4.
8. *Cannock Advertiser*, 22 September 1917; 9 March 1918.
9. Mid-Staffordshire Appeals Tribunal Case 310.
10. Case 736; Case 1067.
11. Case 215.
12. Case 1747; Case 1936; Case 2087.
13. Eustace Joy correspondence, C/C/M/3/8; Case 2116.
14. *Tamworth Herald*, 8 May 1915; Eustace Joy correspondence, C/C/M/4/1.
15. Challinor & Shaw papers, D 3359/64/1; Case 972.
16. *Cannock Advertiser*, 22 July 1916; *Lichfield Mercury*, 23 November 1917.
17. *Staffordshire Advertiser*, 19 January 1918.
18. *Walsall Observer*, 15 May 1915.
19. *Walsall Observer*, 29 May 1915.
20. *Leek Times*, 1 April 1916; 17 February 1917; 24 February 1917; *Tamworth Herald*, 19 May 1917.
21. *Staffordshire Advertiser*, 14 April 1917.
22. *Staffordshire Advertiser*, 21 April 1917.
23. *Staffordshire Advertiser*, 23 June 1917; 2 September 1916.

24. *Staffordshire Advertiser*, 18 December 1915; 6 October 1917; 3 August 1918; *Cannock Advertiser*, 31 August 1918.
25. Case 1887; Case 1406.
26. *Staffordshire Advertiser*, 20 October 1917; *Tamworth Herald*, 20 January 1917; Case 257.
27. *Walsall Observer*, 19 January 1918; *Staffordshire Advertiser*, 3 June 1916; 3 March 1917.
28. *Walsall Observer*, 17 June 1916; *Staffordshire Advertiser*, 7 April 1917; 4 May 1918; 30 March 1918.
29. *Staffordshire Advertiser*, 18 September 1915; 13 July 1918; 8 April 1916.
30. *Tamworth Herald*, 9 January 1915.
31. *Staffordshire Advertiser*, 18 December 1915; 12 October 1918.
32. *Staffordshire Advertiser*, 19 January 1918.
33. This profile is drawn from the files of George Astles, James Coe, Joseph Scott and Frank Maskery, Challinor & Shaw papers, D 3359/64/1-4.
34. *Staffordshire Advertiser*, 9 September 1916.
35. *Staffordshire Advertiser*, 7 April 1917; 23 December 1916.
36. *Tamworth Herald*, 7 July 1917, pp. 33, 48.
37. *Tamworth Herald*, 21 April 1917; *Staffordshire Advertiser*, 31 August 1918.

4. 'Doing Their Bit': Volunteering on the Home Front

1. *Staffordshire Advertiser*, 24 October 1914; 17 October 1914; *Burton Daily Mail*, 2 January 1915.
2. *Staffordshire Advertiser*, 29 June 1918.
3. *Staffordshire Advertiser*, 17 October 1914; 5 December 1914.
4. *Staffordshire Advertiser*, 24 July 1915.
5. *Tamworth Herald*, 5 September 1914, 10 October 1914; 26 December 1914; 9 January 1915.
6. *Tamworth Herald*, 20 October 1917; 18 January 1919.
7. *Tamworth Herald*, 10 July 1915; Lois Turner letters, 5778/1/72, 86; 5778/6/41; *Walsall Observer*, 26 December 1914; *Staffordshire Advertiser*, 3 June 1916; *Lichfield Mercury*, 29 December 1916.
8. *Staffordshire Advertiser*, 1 December 1917; 12 September 1925; Colonel Blizzard's Scrapbook, D797/2/1-3.
9. *Walsall Observer*, 26 December 1914; 29 January 1916.
10. *Walsall Observer*, 10 October 1914.
11. *Staffordshire Advertiser*, 2 April 1920; 26 November 1915; 22 February 1918; *Lichfield Mercury*, 6 May 1921, 24 October 1919.
12. *Staffordshire Advertiser*, 7 July 1917; 20 April 1918; 7 December 1918.
13. *Staffordshire Advertiser*, 27 May 1916; Challinor & Shaw papers, D3359/64/1.
14. *Staffordshire Advertiser*, 16 March 1918; 2 March 1918; 9 February 1918; Edith Birchall diary, 7 January 1918.
15. *Staffordshire Advertiser*, 16 March 1918; 9 August 1919.
16. St Leonards School, Bilston logbook, D836/3; *Staffordshire Advertiser*, 7 April 1917; *Tamworth Herald*, 7 August 1915; *Staffordshire Advertiser*, 11 May 1918.
17. *Cannock Advertiser*, 10 August 1918.
18. Kinver Boys County Primary School logbook, D1408/1/2.
19. *Lichfield Mercury*, 14 February 1919; VAD cards, www.redcross.org.uk; *Staffordshire Advertiser*, 8 November 1919.

20. *Staffordshire Advertiser*, 9 November 1918; 22 March 1919; 14 March 1925; VAD cards, www.redcross.org.uk.
21. *Staffordshire Advertiser*, 15 May 1915; 12 February 1916.
22. *Staffordshire Advertiser*, 2 March 1918.
23. *Staffordshire Advertiser*, 2 February 1918; 11 May 1918; 8 May 1918; 11 October 1919.
24. *Staffordshire Advertiser*, 6 January 1918.
25. *Staffordshire Advertiser*, 25 May 1918.
26. *Staffordshire Sentinel*, 1 February 1916; *Walsall Advertiser*, 31 October 1914.
27. *Staffordshire Advertiser*, 10 November 1917; 14 May 1921.
28. *Walsall Observer*, 20 July 1918.

5. Everyday Life Has To Go On

1. *Leek Times*, 16 January 1915.
2. *Staffordshire Advertiser*, 25 November 1916.
3. *Staffordshire Advertiser*, 24 February 1917; *Staffordshire Sentinel*, 3 March 1917; *Staffordshire Advertiser*, 17 March 1917; 14 April 1917.
4. *Staffordshire Advertiser*, 5 May 1917.
5. *Leek Times*, 28 March 1917; 22 December 1917; *Staffordshire Advertiser*, 22 December 1917.
6. *Staffordshire Advertiser*, 2 February 1918.
7. *Tamworth Herald*, 2 February 1918; *Walsall Observer*, 16 February 1918; *Birmingham Daily Post*, 21 January 1918.
8. *Staffordshire Advertiser*, 22 September 1917.
9. *Staffordshire Advertiser*, 7 July 1917.
10. *Staffordshire Advertiser*, 11 May 1918; 13 July 1918.
11. *Cannock Advertiser*, 8 August 1914.
12. Hints Chadwick County Primary School log book, CEL/22/2; *Tamworth Herald*, 30 June 1917; *Staffordshire Advertiser*, 6 October 1917.
13. *Staffordshire Advertiser*, 18 May 1918; 13 July 1918; *Lichfield Mercury*, 12 July 1918; *Cannock Advertiser*, 5 October 1918.
14. Edith Birchall diary, 21 October 1917, 18 October 1918.
15. Mrs Rose to Eustace Joy, 13 February 1918, C/C/M/4/1/2.
16. *Walsall Observer*, 16 February 1918.
17. *Tamworth Herald*, 9 February 1918.
18. *Cannock Advertiser*, 15 April 1916; *Walsall Observer*, 2 February 1918; 16 February 1918.
19. *Tamworth Herald*, 30 September 1916.
20. Mid-Staffordshire Appeals Tribunal Case 644.
21. Case 736; *Walsall Observer*, 16 February 1918; Case 18.
22. *Leek Times*, 19 June 1915.
23. Case 2111; *Staffordshire Advertiser*, 29 December 1917.
24. Case 759; Case 2035; *Staffordshire Advertiser*, 23 December 1916.
25. *Staffordshire Advertiser*, 1 December 1917; Case 2218; *Tamworth Herald*, 25 August 1917; Case 2212.
26. *Leek Times*, 10 February 1917; *Tamworth Herald*, 17 March 1917.
27. *Burton Daily Mail*, 2 January 1917; *Walsall Observer*, 16 February 1918.
28. *Staffordshire Advertiser*, 18 November 1916; 19 May 1917.
29. *Staffordshire Advertiser*, 14 July 1917; 21 December 1918.

30. *Tamworth Herald*, 24 February 1917; *Staffordshire Advertiser*, 18 August 1917; 31 August 1918.
31. *Tamworth Herald*, 2 March 1918; *Lichfield Mercury*, 6 September 1918.
32. *Staffordshire Advertiser*, 5 January 1918; 7 December 1918.
33. *Tamworth Herald*, 21 April 1917.
34. *Staffordshire Advertiser*, 5 May 1917; 19 May 1917; 26 May 1917.
35. *Cannock Advertiser*, 17 August 1918; *Staffordshire Advertiser*, 12 June 1915.
36. *Birmingham Daily Gazette*, 9 September 1918; *Birmingham Daily Post*, 24 December 1918.
37. *Lichfield Mercury*, 26 April 1918; 6 September 1918; 4 October 1918.
38. *Staffordshire Advertiser*, 29 December 1917; 24 August 1918.
39. *Staffordshire Advertiser*, 16 March 1918; 11 May 1918.
40. *Staffordshire Advertiser*, 27 July 1918; *Walsall Observer*, 16 February 1918; 27 July 1918.
41. *Staffordshire Advertiser*, 19 September 1914.
42. *Staffordshire Advertiser*, 27 November 1915; *Walsall Observer*, 27 February 1915; 1 April 1916; 4 August 1917.
43. Case 1718; *Staffordshire Advertiser*, 3 June 1916.

6. Different Experiences on the Local home Front: The Strangers

1. *Leek Post*, 8 August 1914; *Staffordshire Advertiser*, 10 October 1914, 31 October 1914; *Lichfield Mercury*, 11 September 1914.
2. *Cannock Advertiser*, 5 September 1914.
3. *Walsall Observer*, 8 May 1915.
4. *Staffordshire Advertiser*, 15 May 1915.
5. *Tamworth Herald*, 15 May 1915.
6. *Tamworth Herald*, 15 May 1915.
7. *Staffordshire Advertiser*, 22 May 1915.
8. *Tamworth Herald*, 5 June 1915; 12 June 1915.
9. *Tamworth Herald*, 13 March 1915.
10. Mid-Staffordshire Appeals Tribunal Case 362.
11. *Cannock Advertiser*, 13 November 1914.
12. Case 454.
13. Case 455; Case 2468.
14. *Tamworth Herald*, 8 January 1916; 12 September 1931.
15. *Staffordshire Advertiser*, 29 May 1915.
16. *Staffordshire Advertiser*, 12 February 1916.
17. *Staffordshire Advertiser*, 6 July 1918.
18. *Walsall Observer*, 13 July 1918; *Staffordshire Advertiser*, 12 October 1918.
19. *Staffordshire Advertiser*, 3 October 1914.
20. *Staffordshire Advertiser*, 17 October 1914; 31 October 1914.
21. *Tamworth Herald*, 12 December 1914.
22. *Burton Daily Mail*, 20 January 1915.
23. *Walsall Observer*, 11 March 1916; *Staffordshire Advertiser*, 22 May 1915.
24. *Staffordshire Advertiser*, 13 March 1915.
25. *Staffordshire Advertiser*, 24 October 1914; 9 January 1915.
26. Kinver Boys National School log book, D1408/1/2; *Leek Times*, 6 February 1915; *Walsall Advertiser*, 31 October 1914; *Staffordshire Advertiser*, 5 February 1916; 24 April 1915.

27. *Staffordshire Advertiser*, 1 July 1916.
28. Alexander Maes to vicar of Knutton, 19 February 1931, 6597/1.
29. *Staffordshire Advertiser*, 16 December 1916; 2 February 1918; *Tamworth Herald*, 1 February 1919.
30. *Staffordshire Advertiser*, 17 May 1919.
31. *Staffordshire Advertiser*, 23 February 1918; *Hawera & Normanby Star* (NZ), 8 November 1917; *Staffordshire Advertiser,* 21 December 1918; 20 December 1919.
32. *Dominion*(NZ), 29 April 1919.
33. *Star* (NZ), 12 May 1919.
34. *Staffordshire Advertiser*, 1 June 1918; 8 June 1918.
35. *Staffordshire Advertiser*, 19 January 1918; 26 January 1918; 14 June 1919.
36. *Staffordshire Advertiser*, 31 October 1914.
37. *Staffordshire Advertiser*, 8 June 1918.
38. C. J. & G. P. Whitehouse, *A Town for Four Winters* (Staffordshire County Council, 1983), pp.34–5.

7. Different Experiences on the Local Home Front: Troublesome Locals or 'the Enemy Within'

1. Mid-Staffordshire Appeals Tribunal Case 33; *Lichfield Mercury*, 24 March 1916; 25 May 1916.
2. *Lichfield Mercury*, 16 October 1914; 19 July 1918; Cyril Pearce Register of COs (livesofthefirstworldwar.org).
3. Case 145; *Burton Mail*, 1 May 1916.
4. Case 566.
5. Case 2473; Case 236; *Cannock Advertiser*, 18 March 1916; *Staffordshire Advertiser*, 21 April 1917; 14 July 1917; 18 August 1917.
6. *Tamworth Herald*, 29 April 1916.
7. Case 143; Cyril Pearce Register of COs.
8. *Walsall Observer*, 11 March 1916; *Staffordshire Advertiser*, 22 July 1916.
9. *Walsall Observer*, 11 March 1916; 25 March 1916; 1 April 1916.
10. *Walsall Observer*, 18 March 1916; 1 April 1916.
11. *Staffordshire Advertiser*, 25 November 1916; *Walsall Observer*, 4 August 1917; 6 October 1917; *Staffordshire Advertiser*, 6 July 1918; *Walsall Observer*, 7 December 1918.
12. Case 566; Cyril Pearce Register of COs.
13. *Labour Leader*, June 1917.
14. Cyril Pearce Register of COs.
15. *Burton Daily Mail*, 18 June 1917; 4 June 1917.
16. *Burton Daily Mail*, 24 April 1917; 5 July 1915; *Daily Herald*, 20 June 1914.
17. Case 566; Case 1334; *Staffordshire Advertiser*, 22 July 1916.
18. *Staffordshire Advertiser*, 5 August 1916.
19. Helen Wedgwood to Rosamund Wedgwood, 17 June 1916, JCW/9; Helen Wedgwood to Catherine Marshall, 13 August 1917, Catherine Marshall Papers, D/MAR/4/22, Cumbria Record Office; Interview with Helen Bowen Pease (née Wedgwood), 1976, IWM (www.iwm.org.uk/collections/item/object/80000815).
20. A. J. P. Taylor, *A Personal History* (Atheneum, 1983), pp.36-7.
21. National Council for Civil Liberties papers, The National Archives, KV 2/665.
22. Helen Wedgwood to J. C. Wedgwood, 24 March 1916; J. C. Wedgwood to Rosamund Wedgwood, 8 May 1916, JCW/9.